Claudia Stein

Tel Aviv
The Travel Guide

Claudia Stein

Tel Aviv. The Travel Guide

Managing Editor: Sherrill Layton

Cover Design: Ivan Bogod

Copyrights © 2013 by Contento De Semrik
and Claudia Stein

ISBN: 978-965-550-172-8

Senior Editors, Producers & International sole distributor:
Contento De Semrik
International Publishing House
22 Isserles, 67014 Tel-Aviv, Israel
semrik10@gmail.com
www.semrik.com

Claudia Stein

Tel Aviv

The Travel Guide

Contento De Semrik

Table of Contents

Preface

T EL AVIV STILL REMAINS one of Israel's hidden gems. This is
where modernity merges with Levantine traditions; the city
celebrated its 100th birthday in 2009 and is home to the world's most
extensive collection of International Style buildings. The history of
the Jewish immigrants who followed their vision of a Jewish state
that would give them protection and unite the Jewish people can
still be traced. Only a bit more than little over two decades ago,
the people of Tel Aviv discovered what precious heritage they have
and started preserving it. Today the city is finally presenting itself
to international tourism, and with growing success.

The Israeli seat of government is located in Jerusalem, but Tel Aviv
is the economic center of the country. The city is young and so are
its citizens. Being Jewish is part of their identity but generally the
Tel Avivians are not necessarily religious; which makes it attractive
to those tourists who are looking for a new experience of Israel off
the beaten Biblical path.

This travel guide invites you to beautiful beaches, historical witness,
fascinating architecture, cultural fusion of Orient and Occident
and the busy nightlife of Tel Aviv, a city that never stops.

Tel Aviv, 2013   http://www.telavivstein.com
Claudia Stein   Facebook: TelAvivStein

1
In a nutshell

1.1   Israel

Official Name: Medīnat Yisrā'el = State of Israel
Telephone Country Code: +972 mobile phones +972-5
Internet: .co.il
Time Zone: UTC +2
Currency: New Israeli Shekel (NIS), 1 NIS = 100 Agorot (Sing.:
Agora), ca. 0.20 EUR.
Founding of State: 5 Iyar 5708 (14 May 1948)
Form of Government: Parliamentary republic
National Independence Holiday: 5. Iyar
Capital and Seat of Government: Jerusalem
Official Languages: Modern Hebrew (Ivrit), Arabic
Population: ca. 7,765,700 (2011)
Area: 22,072 km² / 8,522 mi² (without autonomous regions)
Religions: Judaism (75.3%), Islam (20.5 %), other (4.2%)
National Anthem: HaTikwa (Eng.: "The Hope")
Biggest City: Jerusalem (ca. 775,000 residents)

1.2   Short Bio of Tel Aviv

Official Name: Tel Aviv-Yafo
Telephone City Code: 03
Founded: 11 April 1909 as Ahuzat Bayit
Area: 51.4 km² / 19.9 mi², metropolitan area: 1,516 km² / 585 mi²*
Population: ca. 400,000 (city center)
ca. 3.3 million (metropolitan area)
Religions (municipal area): Judaism 91%, Islam 3%, Christianity
1%, other 5%
Mayor: Ron Huldai (since 1998)

*For comparison: Berlin 890 km² / 343 mi², New York 1,213 km² /
468 mi², Paris 105 km² / 40.7 mi².*

General Information

2.1 Security in Israel

IN TODAY'S POLITICAL CLIMATE where terrorism is a general concern in nearly every place of the world, how safe a trip to Israel will be is difficult to say. Israelis are very aware of the threats and have high-level safety measures in place: there is no shopping mall, bus station or parking lot where bags or the trunk of a car will not be inspected; even at the supermarkets you have to open your bag to the security staff (unlike other countries where the concern is much bigger about what you take out than what you bring in). Basic rule of thumb: stay away from the borders; you might get involved in conflicts even though you were not the target. There are more ways to get to the Red Sea than along the Egyptian border. The Gaza strip is really a heavily contested area and it would be extremely ill-advised to include it in your sightseeing plans. It would be best not to even get close as the rockets from Gaza to Israel have become part of daily life in that area, unfortunately. If you really have to visit the West Bank, it will be much safer to go together with a local person. Remember: if something happens to you in these territories, even your embassy might not be able to help. It is always good to call them before you go there and inquire about t'   urrent situation. Beware of the opening hours of the borde: order checkpoints are also subject to closing without prior notice for security reasons. Crossing the border with an Israeli car is risky; you are a target while a foreign car in Israel is not of concern. Your car rental agreement might already waive the possibility to visit other countries with this car. It is also better to drive during daytime.

An unattended piece of luggage is always of great concern. If you discover one, please tell a local person about it.

2.2   Emergency Numbers

T EL AVIV IS A vibrant cosmopolitan city and you should not do anything you would not do anywhere else. Common sense is all you need in this city which is not more dangerous than Paris or Madrid, actually less. Foreign tourists are considered easy victims all around the world and especially women might think twice about how much they show, just like elsewhere in the Middle East. In the unlikely case that something happens to you and you have access to a phone, these are the emergency numbers to call (only work from Israeli phones):

Police: 100
Ambulance: 101
Fire department: 102

2.3   Health Care and Emergencies

I SRAELI HOSPITALS HAVE A very good reputation. If you urgently need a doctor during your stay in Tel Aviv you can go to the Sourasky Medical Center (the former Ichilov General Hospital). This highly modern center is home to three different hospitals and is one of the best in the country. Normally, you have to pay for immediate treatment on site and all credit cards are accepted. If it is not an emergency, your embassy can provide you with a list of doctors who speak your language.

Tel Aviv Sourasky Medical Center
10 Weizman St.
Tel. 03-697-4444 http://www.tasmc.org.il

The **Dental Clinic** is open 24 hours:
18, Reines St. / Frishman St. Tel. 03-523-9241

Pharmacies
There are plenty of pharmacies all over Tel Aviv and you will not have a hard time finding one except for Saturday (Shabbat) and holidays. The following belong to the pharmacy chain *SuperPharm* and are generally open on Saturday from 08.00 to 20.00 hrs (no guarantees). You can also consult the English edition of the local newspapers, like *The Jerusalem Post*, to see which pharmacies are open.

129 Dizengoff/Gordon St.
49 Sderot Yerushalyaim/Oley Zion St.
115 Allenby/Lilienblum St.

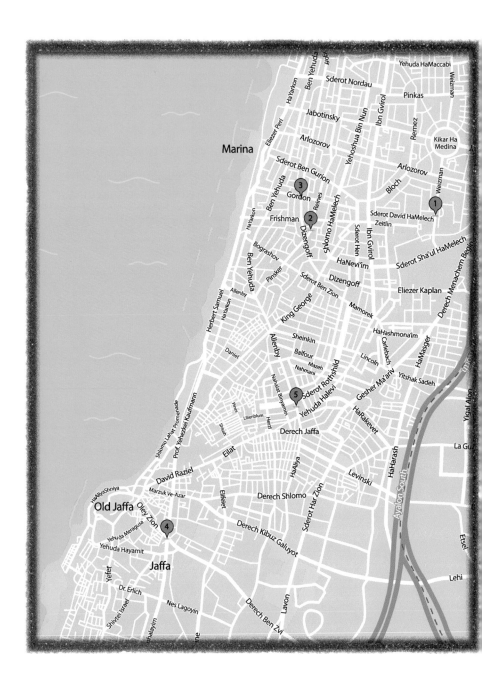

2.4 Good to Know!

Immigration

Tourists need a passport that is still valid for at least six months from the date of their departure. For tourists from many countries, there is no need to apply for a prearranged visa and visitors are allowed to stay in the country for up to 3 months. Please consult with the Israeli Embassy to determine if your country participates in the Visa Waiver Program. Holders of non-machine readable passports will always need a prearranged visa, however. If you want to stay longer in Israel you can apply for an extension at the Israeli Ministry of Internal Affairs. Information is available at their website:

http://www.mfa.gov.il/MFA/About+the+Ministry/Consular_affairs/Visas.htm

Departure

Please make sure you are at the airport at least 3 hours before departure. Due to high-level security measures you will be interviewed about your stay before check-in, the luggage will be x-rayed and frequently also manually inspected.

Ben-Gurion-Airport
General information Tel. 03-975-5555
Arrivals, departures Tel. 03-972-3333
www.iaa.gov.il

Official tourist information - Tel Aviv-Yafo
The city hall is now operating three offices in the city.
Tel. 03-516-6188
http://www.visit-tlv.com
tourist.tlv@barak.net.il

City Center (close to Allenby St)., 46 Herbert Samuel St. / Geula St.
1 November until 31 March: Sun.-Thu. 09.30-17.30, Fri. 09.00-13.00
Closed on Sat. and holidays
1 April until 31 October: Sun.-Thu. 09.30-18.30, Fri. 09.00-13.00
Closed on Sat. and holidays

HaTachana (old train station in Jaffa), Yehezkel Koifman St.
Sun.-Thu. 10.00-20.00, Fri. 09.00-14.00
Closed on Sat. and holidays

Jaffa (at traffic circle, close to Clock Tower), 2 Marzuk ve Azar St.
1 November until 31 March: Sun.-Thu. 09.30-17.30, Fri. 09.30-14.00
Closed on Shabbat and holidays
1 April until October 31:   Sun.-Thu. 09.30-18.30, Fri. 09.30-14.00, Sat. 10.00-16.00
Closed on Jewish holidays.

Embassies
Embassy of the United States
71 HaYarkon St.
Tel. 03-519-7475

Embassy of the UK
1 Ben Yehuda Street
Tel. 03-725-1222

Money
Credit cards are widely accepted for almost any purchase. Most ATMs show the display in Hebrew and switch to English the moment you enter a foreign credit card.

Phone hotlines for credit cards (24/7, only closed on Yom Kippur):
· American Express Tel. 03-636-4445
· Isracard (Visa, MasterCard) Tel. 03-636-4666

If you call from a foreign phone, please substitute +972 for the 0.

Telephone
The City/Area Code of Tel Aviv is 03 (from abroad or a foreign mobile phone, +972-3) and Israeli mobile phone numbers start with 05. If your mobile phone accepts foreign SIM cards, you might consider getting an Israeli prepaid SIM card once you are in the country. The cost of making calls from a local Israeli mobile phone number while in Israel (via an Israeli SIM card installed in your mobile phone) will be considerably less than making them using your home country's SIM card and paying for international roaming charges. In most supermarkets, you can recharge your prepaid SIM card at the cash desk.

Internet
Israel is a high-tech nation and a good Internet connection is considered standard. You will easily find a café with free Wi-Fi. Sometimes, you do not even have to enter the place since the

connection is open without a password and you can simply sit in front on a bench. Throughout the city you will also have the possibility to connect to public Wi-Fi from the municipality. If you do not have your own computer, you can also go to a Internet café; most are also open on Saturday.

Dizi: 13 Ben Ami St. (close to Dizengoff Square)
Log In: 21 Ben Yehuda St. (below Bograshov St).
Interfun: 20 Allenby St. (between HaYarkon and Ben Yehuda St).
Private Link: 78 Ben Yehuda St. / Mapu St. (close to Frishman St).
Web Stop Internet Lounge: 28 Bograshov St. / Hovevey Zion (close to Ben Yehuda St).
Dizi is a nice café that combines a coffee shop and a Laundromat.

Post Offices
In case you want to send something home, please remember that your shipment will be inspected by the customs of your country. Especially in the summer months, this can take a couple of weeks. The following are some centrally located post offices:

3 Zamenhof/Dizengoff Square
170 Ibn Gvirol St. / Sderot Nordau
61 Hayarkon St./ Trumpeldor St.

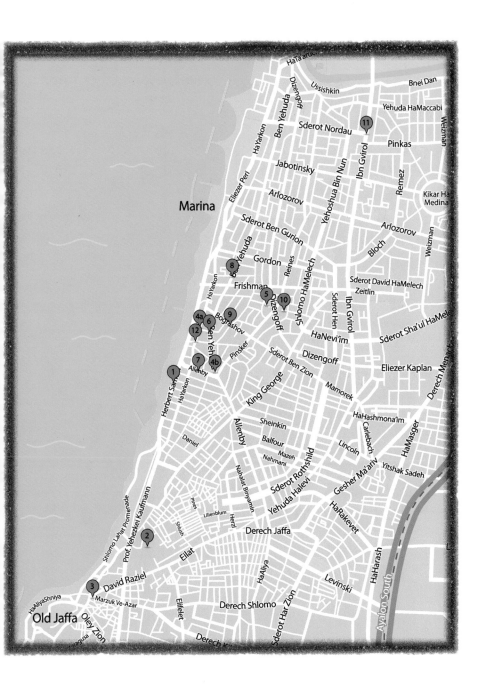

2.5   Holidays

THE OFFICIAL CALENDAR IN Israel is the Jewish calendar. If you are free in your planning, the following holidays might be worth taking into account. For Israelis, it is natural that opening hours are half-day the day before the holiday, they simply forget to tell the tourists about it (e.g. when you want to pick up your car in a location other than the airport).

The most important rule is this: Jewish days start in the evening, including the holidays (*see Genesis 1:5: "And there was evening and there was morning, one day"*). Consequently, *Shabbat* (the Sabbath) starts on Friday evening. The evening when the holiday starts is called *erev* (evening) + name of the holiday; that turns Friday evening into *erev Shabbat*. The correct greetings on a holiday and on Shabbat are *chag sameah* and *Shabbat Shalom*, respectively.

🚕 = taxi, 🚌 = public transport

Shabbat 🚕 yes, 🚌 no

On the seventh day, the Creator decided to rest and this is the belief of the Jews still today. Shabbat is by law a holiday in Israel. Tel Aviv is a very secular city and unlike Jerusalem, many places are open except state-owned or public institutions which normally close on Friday around 14.00. The public transport shuts down Friday afternoon until Saturday late afternoon/evening. Taxis and Mini-Bus Taxis do operate on Shabbat.

For religious Jews, Shabbat is not just the weekend. On Friday evening the "Sabbath Bride" is welcome in the synagogue and next morning, in the presence of at least 10 male Jews, the Torah scrolls are taken out to read the weekly Torah portion. It is a special day where people dress well, spend time with their families, have a nice dinner together and study the Torah. Shabbat ends after dusk. Sunday is the first day of the week and everybody is back to work.

Rosh Hashanah (Jewish New Year) – 1 Tishrei (September/ October) 🚌 yes, 🚆 no

The Jewish year starts in autumn and from 1 Tishrei on, a marathon of holidays takes place, the High Holidays. The ten days from the New Year to Yom Kippur are also called the Days of Awe; atonement and repentance are the main themes. This time of year is very busy in Israel. Many Israelis take holidays to visit their families; Jews living abroad come to Israel for the same reason. The roads are busy and traveling in Israel can be a bit more exhausting than normal. The correct greeting for the Jewish New Year is "Shanah Tovah."

Yom Kippur (Day of Atonement) – 10 Tishrei (September/ October) 🚌 🚆 ♪ no

Nothing happens on Yom Kippur. NOTHING. Life stands still, including the airport and the borders. There is no TV and no radio. Not even taxis or any other vehicle are allowed to drive on the streets that day (except for the fire department and ambulances). Secular Jews make the best of it by enjoying the freedom to cycle on the freeway.

The Days of Awe are a very serious matter. According to the Jewish faith, everybody's destiny is written in a book on the New Year, but this "book of life" will not be sealed before Yom Kippur. In those ten days people are forgiven for everything they have done wrong against G_d and against others. The day of Yom Kippur is spent almost entirely in synagogue services and after 25 hours of fasting, the end of this holiday is celebrated with a rich dinner.

Sukkot (Feast of Tabernacles) – 15 Tishrei 🚌 yes, 🚍 no
It is one of the three Pilgrimage Festivals (later in the Jewish calendar there is also Pesach and Shavuot). Historically, this festival has changed significantly. In the times of the temple, the first fruits of the harvest were sacrificed on Sukkot. After the temple was destroyed, this tradition could not be continued. Today, Sukkot (Hebrew: *sukkah* = hut, *sukkot* = huts) reminds us of the time of deprivation on the way to the Holy Land. Religious Jews build a sukkah in their garden or on their balcony and take all their meals in there. Many even spend the night in them. Most of the Jewish congregations, especially abroad, have one big sukkah for their congregants.

Simchat Torah (Rejoicing of the Torah) – 22 Tishrei (October) 🚌 yes, 🚍 no
The Torah, the five books of Moses, is read every Shabbat in small portions called "parashiyot." At the end of the Jewish year, on Simchat Torah, the last and the first parashah are read. Kids love this holiday: all Torah scrolls are taken out and danced around in a joyous procession, and the little ones get many sweets.

Hanukkah – 25 Kislev (November/December) 🚌 yes, 🚍 yes
The Hanukkah celebrations will be a rather enriching experience for tourists rather than a handicap in their travel planning. During the eight days of Hanukkah, you will see Hanukkah candleholders everywhere (sometimes they are permanent installations) and

people eat jelly donuts (in Hebrew: *sufganyot*), and hash browns (in Yiddish: *latkes*). With fried meals the Jews remember for 8 days the Revolt of the Maccabees in 164 BCE that had led to the re-dedication of the Temple in Jerusalem, formerly desecrated by the Greeks. When they entered the Temple, they found a very small quantity of sacred oil left but it lasted for eight days until new oil had been made.

Purim – 14 Adar (in Jerusalem on 15 Adar, March) yes, yes
If you like Carnival, costumes and theme parties... this is your holiday! All over town you will find Purim parties and people wearing costumes. The biblical book of Esther tells the story of Purim, the salvation of the Jews from the Persian diaspora by Queen Esther who successfully stopped the murder of the Jewish people through Haman (Xerxe's governmental official in

the Persian Empire) who had fixed the day by lot (Hebrew: pur = lot, purim = lots). Alcohol and lots of pastries, "Oznei Haman" (Haman's ears) or "Hamantaschen" are part of the celebrations.

Pesach (Exodus from Egypt) – 15 Nissan (March/April)
🚌 yes, 🚆 no

The second of the three Pilgrimage Festivals might be a little bit more difficult to digest for tourists, though in Tel Aviv many residents simply ignore the prohibition on selling leavened bread and are ready to accept the fine. During this week no yeast product is supposed to be offered, including beer. The traditional Matsot resemble large soda crackers but with even less the taste. The big fast food chains use cornmeal during this week; others just do not sell any kind of bakery products or simply close and go on vacation. There will also be fewer offers for anything that is eaten with pita bread like shawarma and falafel.

This holiday remembers Exodus, the Jewish people's escape from Egypt and the salvation from slavery. There was no time left to bake bread for the journey and for this reason bread and cereals are banned from the kitchen for one week. The first evening is normally spent with family. Together they have a traditional meal that is eaten in a certain order and the "Haggadah" is read (the religious book on the exodus from Egypt).

Yom Ha'atzmaut (Independence Day) – 5 Iyar (April/May)
🚌 yes, 🚆 yes

Independence Day (in Hebrew pronounced: *Yom Ha-Atzma-Oot*) is one of the best times to be in Tel Aviv: beach parties, open-air concerts, decorated balconies... everybody is in a party mood. The official celebrations take place in Jerusalem and can be followed on huge screens broadcasting the festivities. The State of Israel was founded on 5 Iyar 5708 (14 May 1948) in Tel Aviv on Rothschild Boulevard No. 16.

On the day before (called **Yom Hazikaron,** Memorial Day), Israel traditionally commemorates the killed Israeli soldiers. In order to make sure that this day is never on Shabbat, in some years it is artificially moved to another date and so is Independence Day. Another holiday that cannot be on Shabbat is **Yom HaShoah,** the Holocaust Memorial Day (27 Nissan / April). On Yom Hazikaron and Yom HaShoah, sirens sound throughout the country. Everything and everybody will stop; even cars and buses, to commemorate the dead. For one minute, nothing else seems to matter. Israelis expect tourists to do the same.

! The evening of Yom Hazikaron, Yom HaShoah and Yom Kippur (remember: holidays start in the evening,) all café and restaurants are closed. No exceptions. 🚗 🚌 🎵 no

Holidays 2013–2014

	2013	2014
Purim	24 Feb	16 Mar
Pesah	26 Mar	15 Apr
Yom Ha'atzmaut	16 Apr	05 May
Rosh Hashanah	05 Sep	25 Sep
Yom Kippur	14 Sep	04 Oct
Sukkot	19 Sep	09 Oct
Simchat Torah	27 Sep	17 Oct
Hanukkah	28 Nov	17 Dec

2.6 Annual Cycle of Events

February
Jazz Festival, http://www.jazzfest.co.il
Accessible Art Fair, http://www.accessibleartfair.com/tel-aviv

March/April
Días de Flamenco, http://www.keren-adi.org
Marathon Tel Aviv, http://www.tlvmarathon.co.il

May
Felicja Blumental International Music Festival, http://www.blumentalfestival.com
Houses from Within, http://www.batim-il.org

June
Tel Aviv Pride

Bike Station Tel-O-Fun

White Night Festival
Student Film Festival, http://www.taufilmfest.com (every 2 years)
Tel Aviv LGBT Film Festival, http://www.tlvfest.com

July
Opera in the Park, http://www.israel-opera.co.il
Madridanza Tel Aviv, http://www.suzannedellal.org.il

September
Loving Art Making Art

October
SPIRIT Film Festival, http://www.spiritfestival.co.il
Tel Aviv Dance, http://www.israel-opera.co.il

November
Curtain Up Dance Festival, http://www.suzannedellal.org.il

2.7 Public Transport

F IRST THINGS FIRST: ON Shabbat there is no public transport, except mini-vans and taxis. On Friday afternoons just before Shabbat, buses and trains stop operating. Make sure you get to your destination early. During late afternoon / early evening on Saturday, the transport company is back to work.

After your arrival, you can choose between taxi and train to get to Tel Aviv, but there is a considerable difference in price between the two options (e.g. ca. 15 NIS for train and ca. 140 NIS for taxi).

Even though it is very easy to travel around Israel by bus, some places like natural parks or remote beaches can only be reached by car. In comparison to other countries, cars can be rented at reasonable prices in Israel.

Taxi
Tourists should use only the official taxis and make sure the meter is switched on, but this is usually not a problem. Of course, you can negotiate the price with the driver beforehand. The distance between airport and city center Tel Aviv, like Dizengoff Square, will cost you around 140 NIS depending on the traffic. For single travelers, the best deal is the train. When you are leaving Tel Aviv, you can take a taxi or bus to the next train station and then go to the airport by train for ca. 15 NIS. Since there are only shared taxis between Jerusalem and the airport but not from or to Tel Aviv, it is easy to find somebody at the airport who is more than happy to share the ride with you.

> ! In Israel it is not customary to tip
> taxi drivers.

Kastel Taxis
http://www.kastel.co.il
03-6991296/8

Shekem Taxis
03-672-0800
03-527-0404

Bus
You can choose between a single ride ticket, a 10-ride ticket

(kartisiyá) and a day-ticket (Hofshi-Yomi, starts at 9.00 a.m). For the latter, you will receive a rechargeable plastic card (Rav-Kav). With each ticket you can ride for 90 minutes within the city and also change bus lines. The bus tickets do not work for the mini-buses. If you are in the city for longer and think about getting a monthly pass, you will have to get an individual Rav-Kav card with your photo on it. These cards are issued in the offices from the bus lines, e.g. in the New Central Bus Station on Levinsky Street. On the 6th and 7th floor of this not very inviting looking shopping center you will find the offices of EGGED (pronounced *e-gedd*) and DAN, respectively.

Tel Aviv and the neighboring cities belong to "Zone 1," except for Herzliya. With one tariff you can travel quite far, including Rishon Le Zion in the south and Ganei Tikva in the east. Just behind the northern part of Tel Aviv, Ramat Aviv, "Zone 21" starts and a ticket to Herzliya is a bit more expensive than one to Rishon Le Zion.

Sherut

Sherut means service. This is the name for the mini-vans that run from north to south through the city as shared taxis. You can stop them anywhere; not only at the bus station and you can get off any time you like. They also run on Shabbat and late at night.

Train

The train is a north-south connection and is not really important unless you want to go to the University Campus or the airport. Once you leave Tel Aviv though, the train is a great alternative to bus and car and it is by far the most economical way to get from the airport to the city.

Car

This is a special subject: driving. Israel holds a stable position in the world's "top ten" countries for mortal road accidents. The speed limit of 100 km/h on the motorway seems still too high for the Israeli way of driving: Israeli drivers maintain virtually no distance between the cars and the turn signal is only used by newbies and foreigners.

For most tourists, the gasoline stations are a real surprise. In many places you have to go to the cash desk first to make them unlock the gas pump and depending on the oil company, a foreign credit card may only be accepted for up to 200 NIS. If it is not a self-service place, the attendant will type your license number into the computer and ask "Malé?" (full?)

Rental car

As long as you stay in Tel Aviv, having a car is a very painful experience most of the time since parking facilities are not abundant and there are no meters on the street. As a tourist, you will likely end up with a ticket. It is well advised to not pick up your car too early when you plan on leaving town.

The rental companies at the airport provide a shuttle service to their parking lots. If you decide to not give back the car at the airport, make sure you ask when picking up the car where exactly it should be dropped off – signs are rare – and what the opening hours will be at that day. If the next day is a holiday, the office might close earlier than usual. Only the offices at the airport are 24/7.

Parking

In recent years, a car-park routing system has been installed. If you prefer to park your car on the street, you might want to bear in mind this basic rule: if the curb is red, keep driving. It does not matter whether it is red-white, red-yellow or red-gray. Parking could be permitted next to the red-gray area but you have to be able to read the sign with all the exceptions, the same for blue-white. In any case, it is not for free. The municipality has developed a very sophisticated system of display tickets without installing any individual-space parking meters in the street. From 17.00 onward, parking in the street is theoretically only allowed for residents. If you remain parked beyond this time, chances are you will be fined.

Bike

Tel Aviv has only a few bike paths, but biking is very enjoyable here! In no time you can be anywhere in the city and the scenery is amazing. Since 2011, Tel Aviv provides a public bike rental system, Tel-O-Fun. The green bikes are parked all over the city and the system is also open to non-residents. The terminals are also in English and accept foreign credit cards. Alternatively, you can rent a bike from a private rental place. The latter has one advantage that is reflected in the price:

you can come back any time and change the bike or if you have any other problem. Even when the bike has to be replaced after a theft, it is cheaper in a private place than at the city hall.

Some suggestions for bike rental:

Tel-O-Fun belongs to the municipality and provides rental bikes virtually "around every corner" of the city. The price is a combination of membership (minimum 1 day) and rental time. The locations can be found on their website where they also show videos in different languages on how to use the service.

https://www.tel-o-fun.co.il/en
http://www.youtube.com/user/telofun

O-Fun-Bikes is a friendly bike shop with rental service. Their team speaks very good English and they offer different types of bikes. The rental price includes a thick chain with a lock and also a helmet. They also rent child seats and tandem bikes.

197 Ben Yehuda St.
Tel. 03-544-2292
http://o-fun.co.il

Sun.–Thu. 10.00–19.00
Fri. 10.00–14.00

! Closed on Shabbat! Pick-up or drop-off your bike by Friday early afternoon.

At **Cycle Tel Aviv** you can even rent those trailers with which you can dock a kid's bike onto your own and make a tandem. This way you can cycle together safely through the city.

147 Ben Yehuda St. 147
Tel. 03-529-3037
http://cycle.co.il/
Sun.–Thu. 10.00–19.00
Fri. 10.00–15.00

> **!** Closed on Shabbat! Pick-up or drop-off your bike by Friday early afternoon.

Eco Bike offers bike tours throughout Israel but also shorter trips within Tel Aviv (minimum 3 hours). In addition to the "Classic Bike Tour," there is the "Electric Bike Tour" and the "Bike & Beer Tour." All information online: http://www.ecobike.co.il.

Moped
Mopeds or motor bikes can be rented in the following places:

Motogo
19-21 Tushia St.
Tel. 03-681-1717
http://www.motogo.co.il

Motorent
64 Menachem Begin St.
Tel. 03-688-8851/2
http://www.motornet.ybay.co.il
motorent@bezeqint.net.il

3

Urban History

THE OFFICIAL NAME OF the city is Tel Aviv-Yafo. This little
hyphen connects more than just two words; it connects two
different worlds with painful memories. The history of ancient
Jaffa can be well-traced back to the 19ᵗʰ century. Much less was
documented in the last 150-200 years and many of those documents exist only in Arabic, so access to this information by the
western world is limited.

The research of the history of Tel Aviv was also a challenge to
historians but for very different reasons. The history of the city,
which many claim it does not even have, is shrouded in mystery.
Legend has it that it was a suburb of Jaffa that miraculously
became a metropolitan city over the years. Others say that Tel
Aviv had been built by German Jews who fled Nazi Germany,
hence all the Bauhaus buildings.

There are many other versions around but so far, none has told
the historical facts or considered the political environment of
that time which shows the founding of the city in a totally new
and even more impressive perspective. Only in the last 10-15
years have historians, architects and city planners – Israelis and
foreigners –started searching for the traces of the city and its
origins. The wish to get the architecture recognized by UNESCO
(achieved in 2003) reinforced the need for documentation.

At the beginning of the 20ᵗʰ century there were many languages
spoken in the area — English, Hebrew, German, Yiddish, Russian

and Arabic — and therefore, all documents that were finally found were in different languages. Arabic was mainly used, to purchase land from wealthy Arabic owners who mostly did not even live in Palestine and to whom those sand dunes were of little value. The political changes had added another burden to the project. Old maps were the hardest to find and if found, difficult to categorize. Maps and documents from the period of the British Mandate (1918-1948) have practically completely disappeared or had been moved from Tel Aviv to Jerusalem and nobody has ever found them again.

At the same time, it was customary to change street names and personal names to Hebrew. Still today, new immigrants are allowed to change their names once they come to Israel. There are still doubts in many cases if two names on different documents refer to the same person or not.

3.1 Jaffa

A CCORDING TO ONE OF the many legends, Jaffa was founded by Yaphet (Arabic: Yafet), one of the three sons of Noah and one of the eight survivors of the Noachian flood. The exact year is not documented. Excavations have shown that there are eight different settlements below the Jaffa we know today, witnessing roughly 3,800 years of history. It is yet unclear who those settlers were but they were not the same during the whole time; for the last 4,000 years people were moving in and out. The harbor of Jaffa had turned the city into a regional economic center from its earliest years. It had brought the city wealth and international trade relations.

Clocktower in Jaffa

Early in its history, the natural harbor turned Jaffa into an important economic center in the region. The city became rich, cosmopolitan and also the desire of all rulers at that time. The Canaanites, the Philistines, King David and his son King Solomon, Napoleon and the Ottomans – they all had an eye for Jaffa. At the end of the 13th century ACE, after successfully defeating the Crusaders at the harbor, the Mamelukes destroyed the harbor to prevent their enemies from coming back. The Ottomans captured Palestine at the beginning of the 16th century and controlled it until Napoleon arrived in 1799. The area increased in prosperity and the harbor was renewed. During this period numerous Christian pilgrims arrived by boat to Jaffa on their way to Jerusalem. When Egyptian Muhammad Ali Pasha conquered Jaffa, wealthy Egyptian families decided to immigrate. In the following years, Jews from Northern Africa and Turkey also found their way to Jaffa. Slowly but steadily, Jewish life came back again. Those Jews who had already been in the country for quite some time, belonged to the *Sephardim*. Their ancestors had fled from Spain and Portugal and their lifestyle was very eastern. The *Ashkenazim* – from Middle and Eastern Europe – had not been in the country before ca. 1840. Most could not maintain themselves, lived mainly for the study of the Torah and were dependent on payments from the diaspora. When the Ottomans defeated Muhammad Ali Pasha in 1841, Jaffa became an economic center once more. The construction of the Jaffa light house in 1865 was very foresightful, only 4 years later in 1869, the Suez Canal opened and Jaffa became even more important, soon even indispensable: the growing production of Jaffa oranges were exported to many countries.

In the meantime (September 1866) George Jones Adams, founder of the "Church of the Messiah," and his 156 followers had come from Boston to Jaffa. They bought a plot of land, erected the wooden prefabricated houses they had brought from home and started a community in the north of Jaffa that can still be seen today around Bar Hoffman Street. None of them had been prepared for the hardship of agricultural life abroad and only a few months later, in winter 1867 most of them wanted to leave Jaffa and go back home. The majority of them had already left when in the beginning of 1869 some Southern German "Templers" arrived and offered to buy from Adams' group their settlement that would later be known as the "(American-) German Colony of Jaffa." The Templers founded a new settlement east of Jaffa in 1871, Sarona. At the same time there were plans to open a railway connection from Jaffa to Jerusalem and in 1888; the Templers added another little compound close to the future train station. The railway line was opened in 1892.

The construction of the railway confirmed Jaffa's status and brought even more business activities to the city. The old train station, "HaTachana," was renovated a couple of years ago and is now a nice and lively place with coffee shops, restaurants and boutiques. The train station was located in the former urban Arabic quarter of Manshiye that was demolished in the 1960s. In 1870s the first sections of the old city wall were torn down to prepare for future expansion. A new urban district developed in the north of Jaffa, right next to the beach: Manshiye. The Charles Clore Park stands on the former western part of this quarter. The Jewish citizens of Jaffa moved further north and founded Neve Tzedek, Hebrew for "Oasis of Justice," (1887) and Neve Shalom, Hebrew for "Oasis of Peace" (1890). The stand-alone Etzel Museum is one of the last witnesses to history as well as the train station itself,

the Red House next to it and last but not least the Hassan Bek
Mosque. After the demolition the municipality had planned to
erect the Tel Aviv Business District here. But these plans were
later abandoned and today the business district can be found at
the perimeter of Ramat Gan, next to the Ayalon Highway. Other
new quarters from this time are Ajami and JabAliyah in the south
and Souza and Salame in the east. It was a time of a blossoming
economy and more foreigners from many different countries
would immigrate. The Maronite and Coptic Christians started
to populate Ajami where today you can still find many churches
built in those days.

In summer 1914 Hassan Bek became the new mayor of Jaffa
and the mosque of Manshiye – built in 1916 – bears his name.
Bek had a vision; he wanted to modernize the country and the
big and wide Boulevards the Europeans had introduced to the
Middle East served him as a model. After the break-out of World
War I he expelled all Russian citizens from Jaffa. Russia was the
arch-enemy of Turkey and Bek feared conflicts in Jaffa. Those
very Russian citizens were almost exclusively Jewish; hence the
expulsion caused a chorus of outrage among the Jewish com-
munities, including those in Europe. Soon Bek was renowned
for his rigorous and brutal clampdown. Legend has it that he
would arrest people in the street and force them to work for
his city development projects. This course of action also led to
the relocation of some Muslim cemeteries which is against the
religious law. Tel Aviv's Rothschild Boulevard became the model
for Jaffa's Jerusalem Boulevard, at that time named "Jamal Pasha
Boulevard." Jamal Pasha was the governor of Syria since 1915.
After two years in office, Bek was removed.

The "Pioneers' House," a Jewish hostel in Yefet Street, also became one of the targets during the excesses of 1921. An Arabic mob had forced their entry into the house and even local police did not stop them. A Jewish policeman who came by accidentally put the aggressors to flight by the use of his gun. At this point, 14 guests were already dead and the others were hiding on the second floor. A few weeks later the hostel moved to Allenby Street. The consistent assaults provoked the British rulers to broaden the streets in Jaffa to make them easier to patrol with military vehicles; about 250 houses were demolished.

In the two-state-solution, a suggestion from the UN published in November 1947, Jaffa was supposed to be an enclave on Jewish territory. But at this time the two parties were already at war with each other and the UN solution did not seem feasible any longer. The Brits decide to leave Palestine. In November 1947 the first mass exodus set in. About 30,000 Arabs left Jaffa, mainly for Gaza and Beirut. The conflict between Jews and Arabs became even more heated. In January 1948 the Jewish resistance bombed the Saray building, the seat of the Arab administration and End of April the "Irgun" (also called "Etzel") took over Manshiye. In the days following this event the fighters of the Haganah movement conquered the villages outside Jaffa. The British military showed a massive presence in Jaffa but the last 70,000 citizens decided to leave. On 13 May 1948 Jaffa surrendered and the remaining 3,000 people of the former metropolitan city gathered in Ajami. After the founding of the State of Israel on 14 May 1948 the Jews were expelled from the neighboring Arab countries; another mass exodus set in, this time to Jaffa, where only weeks before the Arab population had cast off. They arrived in a deserted town and settled wherever they found a place.

In the 1950s the new developments started in Jaffa and not very much was preserved. Since 1950 Tel Aviv and Jaffa are united and the city's official name is Tel Aviv-Yafo. The many immigrants changed the face of the city and new houses mushroomed everywhere. In the original plans high-rise buildings were supposed to give room to the new citizens; nobody seemed to be interested in preserving anything from the past. Manshiye was completely erased from the landscape in 1963 when the last ruins were demolished. When the harbor of Ashkelon opened in 1965, the golden times of the Jaffa port were finally over and the area became desolate. It was a group of artists who would convince then-mayor Shlomo Lahat in the 1970s to preserve Jaffa. Until today Jaffa is affected by social conflicts, especially because of the rising prices for housing. The recent renovations and new construction attract a wealthier Jewish audience and the local population feels threatened. This forms an excellent arena for Islamic groups. Since 1999 the municipality is investing in the revitalization of Jaffa, a term that does not mean the same to all involved. Today, not much remains of the former Jaffa. The authentic Jaffa can still be found, but only in the hidden little streets, off the beaten tourist path.

Jaffa remains a sore point in the Middle East conflict. Jaffa was the pride of the Arabic population. Why was it abandoned? The reasons are manifold; one is that the Jews had been fed up since the consistent assaults in 1921 and the Arab population feared revenge. The British police had their own daily fight with the Jewish resistance groups and nobody had any confidence in them protecting Jaffa and its population. The Jewish elite had prepared their independence for decades while the Arabs were without a leader or organizational structure. It had been a catastrophe

Dizengoff Tower in Tel-Aviv

– *nakba* – to abandon Jaffa. The "Bride of the Sea" as they called the city, had been the political and cultural cradle of the population. Intellectuals and rich merchants had lived here, where the most important newspapers of Palestine were once published. Feelings of anger, impotence and humiliation come up again when they think of Jaffa.

3.2 Tel Aviv

THE OLDEST AND STILL visible part of Tel Aviv is not Neve Tzedek, it is the Templer settlement "Sarona," locally known as *HaKirya* ("the campus"). After the founding of the State of Israel in May 1948, this area served as the first government seat of the young state. Another settlement – Mount Hope, founded in 1849 – is unfortunately not visible anymore. It was located close to today's motorway junction LaGuardia Interchange in the south of Tel Aviv on the campus of the Shiva Mofet High School (HaMasger Street). The city development has also been significantly influenced by every Aliyah, the Jewish immigration to Israel. On 11 April 1909 the newly acquired plots of land, sand dunes, were split among the new owners and the construction of the first houses began. The motivation for this very project can be best understood in the historical context.

Mount Hope (1849–1853)
In the middle of the 19th century many Christians in the US and Europe were convinced that the Messiah would come back soon. A group of German and American Christians, among them John Steinbeck's German grandparents, came into the country and

together they founded the settlement of Mount Hope in 1849. Their mission consisted of teaching the local Jews agriculture and Christianity. Moses Montefiori, a British-Jewish philanthropist, visited the Holy Land to buy plots of land and finally purchased the Mount Hope orchid plantations from Rabbi Yehuda Halevi. The area is still called the Montefiori quarter. On the night of 11 January 1858, the Christian settlers were attacked by a group of Arabs without any previous incident or warning. The village was looted, some men were murdered and their wives raped. The reasons for this brutal assault have never been identified. Interviewed by the police, the settlers would say that they believe that their successful farming had been the subject of envy among the Arab neighbors. Nevertheless, only a few months later, they would abandon their mission in the Holy Land and move together to the USAT.

The German Templers (1869-1949)

When Tel Aviv started looking into its own young history, the Templers would surface again. They were the group that had most significantly influenced the development of the country and served as a model for the founders of Tel Aviv. They had the most modern houses, applied the latest technology in all their activities and managed to live absolutely independently in the Holy Land. They did not see their mission in teaching Christianity to Jews or Muslims, rather being a living example by living an exemplary life, preferably in the Holy Land, the home of Jesus Christ. This is how they had defined their goal when they split from the National Church in 1861. Christoph Hoffmann (1815-1885) and his followers founded their own church – The Temple Society – in Kirschenhardthof, a village 40 km north-east of Stuttgart in Southern Germany (Baden-Württemberg). The

Templers are often mistaken for The Knights Templar, a Christian military order that was active in the 12th century and responsible for the Crusades, but they have nothing more in common than the name. In 1867 a small group from Germany did not want to wait any longer and decided to move to the Holy Land, without any support from the other Templers. They settled in the Jezreel Valley in the north of the country, between the Galilee and Samaria – a fatal decision. In this sparsely populated area most of them would die in the following years, mainly from malaria. After this tragedy the Temple Society planned very carefully and strategically where to move. The following settlements were finally realized:

Haifa: 1869
Jaffa: 1869 (purchase of the American settlement)
Sarona: 1871 (purchase of 60 hectares of non-arable land from Arabic owner)
Neuhardthof: 1888 (extension of Haifa)
Walhalla: 1888 (extension of Jaffa)
Rephaim: 1873 (close to Jerusalem)
Wilhelma: 1902 (today Bnei Atarot)
Bethlehem: 1906

After the purchase of the American settlement in 1869, the Templers bought the plots that were later known as Sarona, east of Jaffa. Today Kaplan Street crosses the former Sarona and connects Dizengoff Square with the Azrieli Center and its surrounding business district. At the end of the 19th century people from all over would immigrate to Palestine; Muslims, Jews, Christians, but none of these groups invested so much of their energy and knowledge into the future of this geographical area. The Templers stood out. The hygienic situation of Palestine was a challenge for every-body, but especially for the new immigrants, illnesses like malaria made it even worse. The Sarona plots were especially difficult to cultivate and many were sick. The Templers decided to import eucalyptus trees to drain the swamps. The layout of Sarona was planned strategically: the purchased plots were divided into lots, the new owners determined by lottery. Everybody had enough space to build a home with a little garden. The construction was subject to previously determined rules. Interestingly enough, this was not the last "creative urban planning"; the founders of Tel Aviv would do exactly the same in April 1909: subdivide the plots, establish rules for construction and determine the owners by lottery. The founders of Tel Aviv had studied the Templers very closely, especially their buildings were considered all-time modern. Everywhere in the country where the Templers were active, the general living conditions improved in a short time for everybody living in that area. This was the main motivation for Arabs from other areas to move here. From the Templers they learned efficient agriculture or found work on their plantations. The Templers were completely independent. They cultivated their own oranges, fruits, wine, had cattle breeding and dairies. Among the Templers, all kinds of professions could be found and their specialists and skilled workers were very popular and busy outside the Temple Society.

During the economic boom Jaffa started expanding outside the original city walls and also the Templers kept an eye out for new plots. They found a well located area right on the border between Neve Tzedek and Jaffa near where the train was supposed to run in the near future. Here they built their industry (e.g. the water pump factory of Wilhelm and Georg Wagner) and some housing.

The Templers were proud Germans but they considered Palestine "home." None of them had ever thought of going back to Germany; they had invested so much energy and money here, giving up was simply not an option. Since they had dissociated themselves from the German National Church they did not get financial help from anybody, unlike other Christian missions. The reclaiming of the plots and the life they had built was their very own success and they felt like they were a part of the country. Until the end of 1917 Palestine was ruled by the Ottomans. The Turks were quite suspicious of foreigners and other religions but the Templers refused the Ottomans' offer to exchange their German passports for Turkish ones even though this could have gained them many advantages in daily life, especially when permits were needed. On the other hand the Ottomans recognized the Templers' expertise in many areas like the British later did. Several bridges and train stations in Palestine were built by the Templers' engineer Josef Wennagel.

At the end of World War I the British had defeated the Ottomans and life would dramatically change for the Templers, gradually leading to the end of their existence in Palestine. The British accused them of spying for Germany and Turkey and decided to deport them. Most of them would spend the following two years in Helouan, close to Cairo, Egypt. Back in Palestine they would find their settlements in a deplorable state. Their houses were looted, the factories and plantations neglected. Nevertheless, the Templers rolled up their sleeves and built it up once again.

In the 1920s more and more Jews immigrated to Palestine, some following the Zionist dream, others fleeing the uprising anti-Semitism especially in Eastern Europe. This development would lead to even more resentments among the Arab population who felt seriously threatened by the Jewish salesmanship which resulted in an increasing number of assaults against Jews. The Templers remained neutral. They needed the Arab labor and the Jewish clients, but their German nationalism helped the Nazi party (NSDAP) undermine the community. The keeping of German traditions was the perfect stepping stone for the introduction of Nazi ideology which caused tensions among the Templers. Not every Templer was by definition pro-Nazi only because he worshipped in German and wanted to keep national traditions alive. Many saw a contradiction between Nazi ideology and Christian teaching. But most of them did believe that a strong Germany would be helpful for Germans living abroad. In this context it is no surprise that there would later be groups of the Hitler Youth (Hitlerjugend) in Jaffa, a shock for those Jews who had barely escaped Nazi Germany and hardly made it to Palestine because of the British immigration quota that was intended to appease the Arab population and keep all options open in the Middle East where oil had been found. Sarona was located outside Jaffa and most of the time the Templers would take a Moped or a bike to Jaffa. How could they show the Arab snipers that they were not Jews? The Nazi flag with the swastika was well understood.

With the beginning of World War II and the involvement of the United Kingdom it was time to act on the British Mandate of Palestine. The Templers were only good for one reason: they supplied the British with good food including excellent wine, but they were Germans and Germany was the enemy. It was simply unacceptable having the enemy in their own territory. At the same time the overall situation in Palestine became ungovernable: the Jews were hostile against the German Templers because of their affinity with the Nazis, the Arabs attacked the Jews – and also often the British as an expression of their disappointment that their collaboration against the Ottomans had not brought them the promised independence. The British decided to start with the Templers though they had no idea where to deport them; most of them were born in Palestine.

The Wagner family belonged to those Templers who had already been pro-Arab in 1921 during the Arab assaults. Later they would openly sympathize with the Nazis. Even though they had also been interned in an enemy aliens' camp, the British allowed them to re-open their factories after 1945. The Jews were outraged; after the war the atrocities of the Nazis were known all over the world. In March 1946, Gotthilf Wagner was murdered on Levanda Street. The authorities suspected a Jewish resistance group behind this unsolved murder case.

In the following years the deportees were shipped from one camp to another and back to Sarona, only few deciding to move to Germany. In 1948 they are finally transported to Famagusta, Cyprus, and later, in 1948, to Australia.

First Aliyah (1882–1903)
The first Aliyah of the Zionists would ultimately overwhelm Jaffa. Haifa and Jaffa were the only harbors on the shallow coastline and therefore, the first arrival place of all immigrants from which many of them would not want to move on. The ancient city with its narrow little streets was soon about to collapse. The housing shortage was severe and hygiene practically absent; the lack of a sewage system would make things even worse. Living in Jaffa would soon turn into a realistic threat to one's health. The

European Jews in particular could not see themselves adapt to this kind of life. A group of wealthy Sephardic Jews decided to build a new settlement outside Jaffa and bought plots of land. In 1887, the first Jewish settlement outside Jaffa was founded: Neve Tzedek (Hebrew for "Oasis of Justice") and in 1890, Neve Shalom (Hebrew for "Oasis of Peace") would follow. The latter was built right next to Neve Tzedek for the less wealthy.

Herzl and the dream of "The Jewish State" (1896–1904)
Theodor Herzl (1860–1904), in Israel *Binyamin* Herzl was an Austro-Hungarian writer and journalist and is considered the founder of international Zionism. When his book "The Jewish State" (in German "Der Judenstaat") was published in February 1896, in Vienna, nobody could have even dreamed that this was the blueprint of the Jewish State to come and not only an essay on Zionism. Herzl's description of the Jews' misery, the necessity for their own state and his vision on the future political development is so much beyond belief as is the timeliness that is impressed on today's reader. Herzl draws a blueprint on how to establish a Jewish state and most of it was realized in the exact same way, here in Tel Aviv. It was the first Jewish city, founded by Jews and constructed by Jews for Jews. It was the first capital of Israel and a test field for everything to come. Nearly all institutions that were founded with the aim of the establishment of a Jewish state were located in Tel Aviv. Here the corner stones were laid for a new Jewish society; a free society, independent from non-Jews and self-determined, not reduced to its religion but recognizing the religious values as its pillars. Many of the European Jews were not very religious but the society they lived in and for which they had fought in wars did not integrate them; they were simply Jews. Herzl described it in the following way:

Attacks in Parliaments, in assemblies, in the press, in the pulpit, in the street, on journeys--for example, their exclusion from certain hotels--even in places of recreation, become more numerous daily. The forms of persecution vary according to the countries and social circles in which they occur. In Russia, imposts are levied on Jewish villages; in Romania, a few persons are put to death; in Germany, they get a good beating occasionally; in Austria, Anti-Semites exercise terrorism over all public life; in Algeria, there are traveling agitators; in Paris, the Jews are shut out of the so-called best social circles and excluded from clubs. Shades of anti-Jewish feeling are innumerable.

The book provoked very different reactions among Jews and non-Jews but what annoyed Herzl most was that it would be classified as utopia. His book picks up the "Jewish Question" that – according to Herzl – has not been given a solution since the Middle Ages. At the end of every Pessach celebration Jews say "Next year in Jerusalem!" Since the destruction of the Second Temple in the year 70 CE and the Romans coming into power, the Jews have been dreaming of coming back to their country and to found the State of Israel in the Land of Israel. Even in times of uncertainty and prosecution the Jews always hesitated to leave the country they were living in; they simply did not know where to go and this would not change if they did not have their own State. Herzl drew a concrete and detailed roadmap that was based on two pillars: the *Society of Jews* and the *Jewish Company*. He also suggested several ways to finance this project.

The task of the *Society of Jews* was primarily to build the nation and to prepare the political and economic conditions while the *Jewish Company* should take care of their execution. Palestine was chosen as this future home due to the historic Jewish ties to this piece of land. According to Herzl the land was the only resource that required approval from outside the community. He was confident that those countries with strong anti-Semitism would happily support a Jewish state. He knew that the country was mostly not arable. He suggests that the poorest of the poor immigrate first. They had never lost their belief in the Holy Land and nothing tied them to their country of residence except misery. Russia and Romania seemed to be ideal for the first recruitment.

The main tasks of the *Jewish Company* were the acquisition of land under private law that later should be guaranteed under international law. The workers would construct their shared residences for each other; simple and functional accommodation. The apartment block in Frishman Street 33-35 is an example of those days. Those workers were supposed to build up the whole country, starting with the residence and continuing with the infrastructure. An incoming agency would filter the stream of immigrants and they would settle next to their work. The remaining Jewish assets that could not be taken to Palestine would be listed for potential sale to Christians.

At the end of August 1897, Herzl held the World Congress of Zionism in Basel where the *Basel Program* was agreed: "Zionism seeks the creation of a secure home for the Jewish people under public law." On 3 September 1897, Herzl wrote into his diary: *"If I summarize the congress of Basel in one word – which I will be wary of saying out loud in public – it will be this: in Basel I founded the Jewish State. If I said that in public I would face a broad laughter. Maybe in 5 years, but definitely in 50 years, they will all agree."*

In 1902, Herzl published another script with the title "Altneuland" – Old New Land. It was meant to be a brochure for non-Jews with which Herzl wanted to promote the advantages he saw in the emigration of his people to the Holy Land. His vision for the next 20 years included modern technology, streets, embankment dams, irrigation systems and a peaceful co-existence with non-Jews who would greatly benefit from the modernization the Jews bring to the country. "If you will, it is no dream" – an often-quoted citation from "Altneuland" that became the slogan of Zionism.

Second Aliyah (1904–1914)

This is one of the most important periods in regard to the founding of Tel Aviv. It is the time when the founding fathers immigrate. Still today the historians are wondering if "Ahuzat Bayit" as Tel Aviv was called at the beginning, was meant to be only a suburb with little nice gardens or whether this was only the embryo of the already imagined Jewish metropolis à la Herzl, a Jewish city for a Jewish state. We will never know. But it is a fact that Tel Aviv was not founded to leave Jaffa, this is what Neve Tzedek and Neve Shalom were for. The immigrating Europeans from places like Odessa, Kiev, Berlin and Budapest could simply not adapt to the mid-eastern way of life. In 1904, the Kerem HaTeimanim (vineyard of the Yemenites) neighborhood was founded by immigrants from Yemen. They were Zionists, too, but not in a political way and their lifestyle was more in tune with the mid-eastern culture.

Under the auspices of Akiva Aryé Weiss the building society "Ahuzat Bayit" was founded in 1906 with the main purpose of building this new suburb of which the Europeans had been dreaming. The current Jewish suburbs were too eastern to fuel immigration from Europe: still no sewage system, the streets were dirty and most public spaces neglected. The settlement of the Temple Society, Sarona, was a model the founders studied meticulously. Sarona was the embodiment of modernity and it had a European look and feel. It was no wonder that on 11 April 1909, the distribution of the lots of land to the first 66 families had been organized the Templers' way. The rules for the new owners were similar. They were allowed to build as they liked on their own piece of land with only a few restrictions, for example only one third of the space could be built on. For the public spaces, it was necessary to appoint an architect. Like the Templers, the Ashkenazim had little relation with the sea and started to flatten the sand dunes with their back to the water. The first building was finished in October 1909, and in 1910 the suburb was renamed "Tel Aviv," the title Nachum Sokolow had given the Hebrew translation of Herzl's book "Altneuland."

The most prominent founding fathers were Meir Dizengoff (1861-1936, originally from Moldavia) and Akiva Aryé Weiss (1868-1947 from Belarus). Dizengoff came to Jaffa in 1905. The charismatic and handsome business man soon gained influence in Jewish society. He invested in many different fields and would soon start buying plots of land outside Jaffa. Weiss arrived in Jaffa in 1906 coming from Łódź, Poland. He was determined to execute Herzl's plan; a Jewish society needed a Jewish city. In his opinion the agricultural settlements and the embellishment of existing buildings were simply not enough. He envisioned a large Tel Aviv for a new society. The day of his arrival he went to the first local meeting. The popular demand of his ideas resulted in his assignment for the execution. The building society "Ahuzat Bayit" was founded and soon construction of the first buildings started. When "Ahuzat Bayit" was finished in 1910, Weiss could not find any supporters for his plans for expansion and he decided to leave and invest in his own projects. Weiss contributed significantly to the development of the country by founding several factories and companies, like the "Ora Hadasha" movie company. He was also the builder of the "Eden Cinema" and the first post office building of the city. Later he would initiate the "Diamond Club," the embryo of today's Diamond Exchange.

Dizengoff had been cooperating right from the beginning with the "Ahuzat Bayit" society for the purchase of land. In 1911 he became chief city planner and 1922, the city's first mayor. During the following years Dizengoff practically eliminated Weiss from history and promoted himself as the initiator of the city who had smartly led the development from suburb to metropolis. The fact that the first plans for expansions had come from Weiss was omitted as were the main contributions of the Scottish city planner Patrick Geddes.

The British government published the Balfour Declaration on 2 November 1917, shortly after General Allenby had conquered the city of Beer Sheva and ended the Ottoman reign. In the Balfour Declaration the British committed themselves to help the Jews get a national home. During the British Mandate, Jews were allowed to immigrate to Palestine but there was no support available in any other aspect.

Third Aliyah (1919–1923)
The 1st of May 1921 was the day Jews would not forget for a long time. It was the day of Arab assaults on Jewish demonstrators. Two Jewish groups violently clashed during Labor Day demonstrations. The demonstration of the Jewish Communist Party had been authorized, but the Workers' Union (today Israel's Workers' Party, then lead by David Ben-Gurion) had called for an unauthorized countermarch. Both groups were knocking each other around when suddenly an Arab group gathered to beat up the Jews, the violence escalated and lead to shootings and more violence. The Arab Police ignored the incident. The Jews were in shock. The civil population organized themselves and sealed off Tel Aviv. In the days that followed they picked up the remaining Jews in Jaffa and cast out Arabs from Jewish neighborhoods. In the end Jaffa was purely Arabic, an apparent victory for the aggressors that would soon backfire. The "assaults of Jaffa" went on for

three days, but in this first week of May, Jews were attacked by Arabs all over the country. Life would change forever.

After the assault, the British High Commissioner Lord Herbert Samuel soon reorganized the administration: in June 1921, Tel Aviv was granted some autonomy and could impose tax. Until 1923, it was still mandated by Jaffa, later it was gathered with Neve Tzedek, Neve Shalom and Kerem HaTeimanim as well as all the purchased plots. Jaffa, the economic center until then, got cut off and suddenly there was a real gap between clients and merchants. For the latter, it was much more difficult to swallow. The Jews would avoid Jaffa. The new municipality stressed on the expansion towards the Yarkon River in the north – without Arab labor – and opened new shops; the products were imported from Europe and the money, too. Jaffa sank into poverty. The port business "saved" Jaffa until 1933. This was the year when the Haifa port opened and the monopoly fell. The border between Jaffa and Tel Aviv was drawn on Daniel Street, south of the Yemenite Quarter, on the other side of Manshiye. This area was the scene of fights between Arabs and Jews since then, especially in the 1940s.

The development of Tel Aviv benefitted from the events that reminded many citizens of Herzl. Self-supply and the responsibility for the own safety were the immediate tasks to fulfill. All labor became exclusively Jewish and the clichés would disappear. Being able to plan the future had been a Jewish dream for too long and now, for the first time, they had the chance to take care of their own destiny. The new immigrants of the third Aliyah had to live in tents on the plots in the north. The *Palestine Land Development Company* would from now on be in charge of the purchase of new land.

Fourth Aliyah (1924-1929)

These were the golden days of Tel Aviv. The cultural life was booming and well-educated Europeans immigrated. The municipality appointed the Scotsman Patrick Geddes as strategic city planner, a so-far unknown profession. Patrick gave the development the necessary rebound. Until then, all the planning only considered those plots of land that had already been purchased. Geddes would freely draw a new map, disregarding land ownership. He concentrated on large north-south and east-west connections. Geddes was a biologist. He studied closely the relationship between beings, in this case: the citizens. Where did they go, on which routes, who met who? He identified big streets for the main traffic, the access to the houses where wives and mothers interacted were already significantly smaller. The ways to the bakery as well as to the parks were supposed to be short. Here, where mothers and children lived, main traffic should be avoided. Geddes was not Jewish but sympathized with Zionism. Although Tel Aviv was a secular city, they all wanted to live in a society based on Jewish values. They agreed that Jewish holidays would be days off and celebrated in public. Synagogues were not the center of daily life anymore, but still a main part of the culture and, therefore, should be in reasonable reach. Geddes understood the task. He took all those elements together to lead Judaism from religion to culture. Theaters, libraries and boulevards were the new center of public life. He also examined the local climate and the challenges it presented. He was the first in planning cubic houses with roof terraces, not those architects who would later earn their diplomas in Europe. Geddes understood the Jews' search for a new, modern Jewish society and avoiding any impression of tightness. In his planning, he left out a considerable amount of space for green areas. The city was supposed to be light and the buildings should not remind of the European "Shtetls," away from walls and cemeteries. In 1925 he presented a plan in which he planned the city from Bograshov Street up to the Yarkon River, the eastern border was Ibn Gvirol Street.

מועדון־יהלום א"י

PALESTINE DIAMOND CLUB

The original Palestine
Diamond Club sign

From 1927, it became increasingly difficult to get a building permit from the authorities in Jerusalem because High Commissioner Lord Herbert Samuel had been replaced by Lord Plumer. More and more, the Brits would reduce Tel Aviv's newly gained autonomy, especially their finances. From now on, the city expansion had to rely on donations only instead of taxes. At the same time, land to buy was getting scarce and the municipality would pass a new bill that allowed the expropriation of land from owners to win space which was more needed than ever from 1933 onwards.

Fifth Aliyah (1929-1939)

Tel Aviv was finally running out of space and at the same time new immigrants would flood the country. The British bureaucracy for building permits would slow down construction activities, the rest of the world was suffering from an economic crisis and not much money was sent to support the projects in Tel Aviv. It had turned into a vibrant, European-style city; most of the new European immigrants did not want to move on to other parts of the country and stayed in Tel Aviv. As a result, it had become impossible to keep all the green areas that Geddes had planned. Even existing gardens and parks had to give way. According to reports from that time, between 1931 and 1935, the population had tripled and reached 120,000. In 1934, the Jewish National Fund was able to purchase new plots of land in the north. Hence, mainly immigrants from Germany and Hungary, where the majority of immigrants came from, would settle in this area. Though all the labor was Jewish, the unemployment rate was very high. The Jewish society would drift apart into European Jews (*Ashkenazim*) and Eastern Jews (*Sephardim*). The *Ashkenazim* would live in the north, the *Sephardim* in the south. This has not changed through today, only the distribution of unemployment is different: today, there are more people in the south without a job. The new immigrants at that time would all go north. The German Jews had the most difficulties adapting. Most of them had been very established with a "normal" life in Germany until the Nazis came to power, so adapting to their new home proved difficult, unlike the Eastern European Jews who had integrated well in the new land and picked up the language very fast. For the "Jeckes" (pronounced: yeckes), as the Germans were called – because they always kept their jacket on, even in the summer heat, and hardly spoke Hebrew – the Eastern Europeans had no respect.

1936 was an emotional year for Tel Aviv and Israel in general. It was the year when the Arabic Revolt started that would not stop until 1939. Their leader was the Grand Mufti of Jerusalem, Mohammed Amin al-Husseini, who was on friendly terms with Nazi Germany and had significantly introduced the idea of anti-Semitism in the Arab world. In Syria and Egypt, the Arab workers had already been successful with their work stoppage and negotiations on their independence from France, and the British Crown had already been on their way.

On 17 May 1936, the works for the new Tel Aviv port started. This was another step towards independence; there was no other harbor between Haifa and Jaffa. The coast is very shallow here and big ships came as close as they could, then the passengers as well as the goods had to be transshipped into small rowing boats. This business was nearly 100% Arab. Since the assaults from 1921, confidence in the Arab neighbors had vanished and nobody could still imagine a peaceful co-existence. These worries were fueled by the massacres from Hebron and Safed in 1929, and the attacks would not stop in the years to come. The landing in the port of Jaffa would take longer with every ship that entered due to increasing immigration and the expansion of the local economy. Oftentimes, the ships would have to wait for several days for their unloading. On 13 December 1934, two ships collided with each other close to the Yarkon estuary in the north; hence, a lighthouse was built in January 1935, close to today's port. A new port was the only solution. The name of the street closest to the port refers to those days: "Shaar Zion Street," the gate of Zion. In 1949, the municipality started an expansion of the Tel Aviv harbor by deepening it. This way, ships could enter the port and did not have to be unloaded at sea. The Grand Mufti ended the Arab strike in October 1936, and one month later the British would found the *Peel Commission* to investigate the Arab Revolt.

1936 was also the year the municipality constructed the Ben-Gurion airport between Tel Aviv and Jerusalem that would initially be open only for military usage.

The Peel Commission declared in July 1937 that the strong anti-Semitism among the Muslim population could lead to only one possible solution: the separation into two states. Even though the Jewish part was much smaller and the Arabs had already been granted the whole territory east of the Jordan River (today known as the "Kingdom of Jordan"), the Arabs refused and the Grand Mufti would start the revolt again. At the end of that year, there were mass revolts and assaults on Brits and Jews but this time the attackers came from the rural population. The mayor of Tel Aviv, Israel Rokach, asked the British Mandate government for a permit to build an airport for Tel Aviv. Traveling had become a huge risk for Jews. The airport Sadeh Dov was inaugurated in 1938 and offered regular flights to Haifa. The results of the Peel Commission led the British to give major concessions to the Arabs. Most probably, this move was motivated by the Crown's interest in the Middle East and the assumption that the Jews would depend on them. The next steps would be cemented in the "White Paper of 1939": in the following 5 years, only a maximum of 75,000 Jews were allowed to immigrate; any higher number would be subject to Arab approval. At the same, time the purchase of land through Jews became very much restricted.

World War II (1939-1945)

On 9 September 1940, Tel Aviv suffered its first air bombing, and without any prior warning and medical infrastructure in place. It was a hit from Mussolini against the British. The damages were considerable and 137 people lost their lives. Most of the victims were "residents" of the tent settlements that were not even equipped to withstand a major storm. A memorial stone reminds of this incident on the corner of King George Street and Ben Zion Boulevard. Less than a year later, the Vichy regime sent bombs to Tel Aviv; this time 20 people died.

End of the Palestine Mandate (1947-1948)

The British government decided to give up their mandate in 1948. The years of 1948 and 1947 felt like civil war. Jewish resistance fighters and Arab snipers fought each other violently. In December 1947, the Jewish National Fund managed to purchase the Templer compound of Sarona from the Mandate parliament. The municipality had now gained land of an important size. This was not for residential purposes; they were looking for the future government seat of the state they were about to create. The area was renamed *HaKirya*, the campus, and "Sarona" would not be heard or read for a long time. On 5 Iyar 5708 (14 May 1948), David Ben-Gurion formally proclaimed the establishment of the State of Israel. At the end of the same year, the decision was taken to group Jaffa and Tel Aviv in one city which finally happened in 1950.

Until today, there is a still a north-south division in Tel Aviv, though the municipality is trying to modernize the southern districts, including Jaffa, but the local residents simply cannot keep up with the modernization. Rents are rising and many have to give way to residential luxury projects and live in poverty. The protests on Rothschild Boulevard in 2011 have shown that this problem is not limited to only the southern districts anymore.

3.3 Tel Aviv today

Tel Aviv can be roughly divided into 5 districts:

- North
- Northern Center
- Center
- South
- Jaffa

Patrick Geddes had planned the city up to the Yarkon Park, which for a long time was the city's northern border. Today, the **North** stops where Herzliya, the next city, begins. The stylish towers with its condominiums for the wealthier residents as well as the University are located north of the Park. Locals call the part between Ben-Gurion Boulevard and Yarkon Park the "old North," though correctly this would only apply to the area west of Ibn Gvirol Street. Geddes' plan had not included the areas further east. The now closed-down Tel Aviv port is also located in the "old North" and offers night life, bars, restaurants, and coffee shops right next to the sea. And last but not least, Dizengoff Street is a very prominent old-time witness with its elegant shops.

The famous Dizengoff Square with its classical International Style architecture is located in the **Northern Center**. Most of the buildings from the 1930s are located here. Between Ben-Gurion Boulevard and Bograshov Street, 75% of the buildings belong to the "White City" as defined by the UNESCO.

Tel Aviv's **center** is rich in history. This is where everything began: the first houses of Ahuzat Bayit and the Rothschild Boulevard were located here, as well as the first Jewish high school. Later, in 1948, the State of Israel was formally proclaimed on Rothschild Boulevard No. 16. The center is also called "**Lev HaIr**" – heart of the city. The streets already existed in old plans from 1924, but some of the houses were constructed later.

The districts of Neve Tzedek and Florentin form the **South.** Shortly before the end of the century, Jaffa had started to expand. The Maronite Christians would found Ajami in the south of Jaffa, the Muslims went north and settled where today the Charles Clore Park can be found and the Jews founded Neve Tzedek. Some 30 years later, Florentin was founded by Greek Jews from Saloniki. The cornerstone for the Kerem HaTeimanim was laid in 1904 but because of its geographic location, it is not part of the South. Jaffa is also south, but it is mostly mentioned apart.

Jaffa, "the beauty," with its medieval history and the exceptional fusion of Arabic and European culture, different religions, and architecture and ethnic food extends to Bat Yam, the next city in the south.

Box Office Cameri Theater

4
Architecture

W HEN TEL AVIV WAS founded in 1909 as *Ahuzat Bayit*, the modern architecture had not yet been designed. The construction left and right of Rothschild Boulevard combined all different kinds of styles. This sometimes "wild" style combination is called *Eclectic Style*. The owners had in mind the houses from the countries they have left behind, adapted this mostly Middle- and Eastern-European style to the trends of that time and the eastern elements they found at site. The pointed windows in the Ottoman style were especially popular. European architects had come to visit Palestine long before the 1930s. They did not come to check out Aliyah possibilities; they were simply attracted by the opportunities this empty piece of land would offer to architects. Tel Aviv was a test field in many areas. City development, as it is known today, did not exist back then. The unrestricted planning of a completely new town was a great chance that would not come back soon. In the 1920s, Tel Aviv blossomed, its cultural scene being as abundant as that in Berlin or Budapest. The city kept growing and new construction surfaced everywhere: movie and stage theaters were built and Europe's intellectuals could not resist the city's charm. The cultural life was booming. The purchased land was rapidly covered with buildings and each time the houses would look more modern. The years of heavy immigration, especially at the end of the 1920 and again after 1948, posed the challenge to rapidly construct cheap residential buildings. Under this pressure, more than one historic building was sacrificed.

When Tel Aviv was awarded the UNESCO World Heritage status on 3 July 2003, nobody would have even dreamed that this would be a tourism magnet of the near future. Even new construction is designed in the International Style again. "Bauhaus" is a term that seems to be intrinsically tied to Tel Aviv. Does this mean that every International Style building is a "Bauhaus"? The document from the UNESCO refers to the "White City of Tel Aviv – The Modern Movement." Tel Aviv is home to over 4,000 buildings from the 1930s, many in a deplorable state. What exactly was "The Modern Movement" in architecture? Different but similar ideas can be identified, but no exact criteria for a definite and clear classification. Some examples:

·   New Building (from German: Neues Bauen)
·   Bauhaus
·   New Objectivity (from German: Neue Sachlichkeit)
·   International Style

New Building
This totally new way of building would be applied mainly between 1910 and the 1930s. The architects would use different, new material – like glass, steel, iron – and pre-fabricated construction elements to create more spacious and especially lighter rooms. This was understood as a counterbalance to the predominant mainly shady backyards and tenement houses. Building was being streamlined.

Bauhaus

In 1919, Walter Gropius founded the Bauhaus school (in German "Staatliches Bauhaus") in Dessau. The principle idea was to unite crafts and the manual arts to create something new that would combine art and production with the final goal to eliminate the society's hierarchies, called "classes." The artist was for Gropius the epitome of the craftsman. The artisan tradition was the base of creation that was finally supposed to lead to a more humane society. During the first Bauhaus exhibition in 1923, the prototype of Bauhaus architecture was presented. In only 4 months, the building "Haus am Horn" (German: house at the horn), designed by Georg Muche, was constructed in Weimar. It was meant to be a livable prototype and first representative of a future settlement for the Bauhaus professors. The whole settlement was actually realized later in Dessau. The building disposed of a simple cube with a functional and sober interior architecture. This was very typical for the beginnings of the involvement of the Bauhaus school in architecture. The Haus am Horn was seen as a representative of the New Building. Already in 1922, Gropius had presented a nowadays renowned sketch for the new construction of the "Chicago Tribune" skyscraper. This "classical Bauhaus building," is characterized with its clear lines and much glass. Unfortunately it was never realized. The one element that can be found in all Bauhaus buildings is the usage of pre-fabricated building parts that can be individually adapted to its final purpose. Building according to the Bauhaus school meant to use a "kit," like honeycomb – as Gropius would say.

The members of the Bauhaus school were considered leftwing and because of their socialistic ideas, they were a thorn in the Nazis' side. After the Nazis won the elections, the Bauhaus school

– now in Berlin because in Dessau they were closed already – was forced to close in July 1933. Many of the members emigrated and continued their work in their new countries, mainly in the USAT. This is how the Bauhaus principles were introduced to the other side of the ocean.

New Objectivity
The term applies to those buildings that were later built in the "Bauhaus Style" but not by a member from the Bauhaus school.

International Style
The architectural historian Henry-Russell Hitchcock (1903-1987) and the architect Philip Johnson (1906-2005) used this term to describe the minimalistic and functional elements of architecture in the 1920s and 1930s. In Tel Aviv, there are about 4,000 buildings that belong into this category.

The influence of Le Corbusier
Le Corbusier (1887-1965) was Ze'ev Rechter's mentor and, therefore, it is not a surprise that the latter would be the first to build a house on pillars (Engel House, 84 Rothschild Blvd), because this was just his mentor's very own signature. In the 1920s, Le Corbusier developed "The Five Points of Architecture": pillars (pilotis), roof garden, free façade (non-load-bearing walls), free floor plan and long strips of ribbon windows. The pillars guaranteed the green area and the roof garden created even more. With the support of the pillars, there was no need any more for supporting walls and all static requirements were abolished and the floor planning became totally free. Consequently, the facades could be opened anywhere and windows did not have to be installed upright anymore, they could also be crosswise.

International Style Building

All five elements can be identified in Tel Aviv within the White City. Together with Max Dubois, Le Corbusier owned a patent for the building of prefabricated houses with steel frame. Tel Aviv's fast development and expansion has benefited greatly from Le Corbusier's inventions. For him, economical and functional construction were a logical answer to the technical progress in the world, that which would result in fast-happening changes in people's environment and lifestyle.

4.1   The White City

T HE WHITE CITY ENCOMPASSES mainly the area south of Ben-Gurion Boulevard, west of Rothschild and Chen Boulevard. The vast majority of the buildings here represent the New Objectivity and the International Style respectively, though Israelis love to present every building as a "Bauhaus." The principles of the Bauhaus school have been applied in many buildings at least partially, e.g. with the roof garden for all tenants, or the workers' residence on Frishman Street 33 where there are big common areas for eating and showing, but no usual apartments. Speedy and economical construction became top priority at the latest by the 1930s when the number of immigrants increased. The prefabricated construction elements were ideal. The Bauhaus school has worked a lot with glass and iron to let light and air into the apartment but in Tel Aviv, the local climate presented its very own challenges. Light was appreciated but sun was not, the building was not supposed to open towards the south and big windows were avoided. Typical for houses in Tel Aviv are the narrow strips of windows. There was no iron production in Palestine and the use of these pricy imported elements was reduced to a minimum, unless it was a private building and the owner was ready to pay for it. Le Corbusier's pillar concept can be found in many buildings, too. It was a great space-saving way to create a little garden when there was actually no space at all for the kind of front garden Patrick Geddes had suggested in his master plan from 1925. Many of the local buildings show a combination of the rectilinear Bauhaus Style and geometric forms. The architects in Tel Aviv used the term "organic architecture." Europeans would have never named it this way since organic architecture for them was just another name for chaos. In Judaism, perfect health is a gift from the creator, hence, also the body and its form. The basic forms – round or edged – create this asymmetry. The masters at the Bauhaus school did not use them in their plans and for this reason; these buildings are clearly of International Style.

"Israeli Box Style"

In the late 1940s, during the struggle for independence, the International Style was minimalized once again. The result was the box. Construction had to be fast, there were no capacities left for any kind of design. This would not change until the mid-1950s. At this time in Israel, more immigrants than ever, poured into country. After the state founding, Israel had to take care of itself and at the same time secure its borders. Also, the box buildings were mostly constructed on pillars, but any other style element that locally is called "typically Bauhaus," disappeared.

Exhibition: Batim MiBifnim

Since 2007, Tel Aviv has been a member of the "Open House Family," an organization that organizes visits and guided tours

in different cities around the globe. Parks, private houses, public buildings and factories open their doors for one weekend. In Tel Aviv, this free Batim MiBifnim festival (Hebrew for "houses from inside") takes place every year in May. Many walks and guided tours are also held in English.

4.2   Architects in Tel Aviv

L EGEND HAS IT THAT Tel Aviv has been built up by German Jewish architects or prosecuted members of the German Bauhaus movement who came to Palestine to realize their ideas. The truth is that the famous architects, who were nearly all from

Eastern Europe, had made Aliyah to Palestine and later went to Europe to study from the local masters. Back in Palestine, they had then constructed in this new architectural language that was not a unique invention from Germany only, but one that was adapted to the local challenges and requirements: climate, socialist ideas and time pressure to build up the country.

Arieh Sharon (Poland 1900, Israel 1984)

Born Ludwig Kurzmann, Sharon came to Israel in 1920. He was a co-founder of the kibbutz Gan Shmuel and in 1928 he decided to study at the Bauhaus in Dessau, Germany. A year later, he got married to Gunta Stölzl, the Bauhaus master of the weaving mill. His style is minimal as can be seen in the workers' residence Meonot Ovdim that is actually an "urban kibbutz" since it has the same structure for the community spaces (laundry, kitchen, mensa, kindergarten, etc). The residence in Frishman Street 33-35 is the best known of his urban works. Sharon developed the blue print for the building up of Israel and was the right hand of David Ben-Gurion. He is considered the father of Israeli architecture.

Dov Karmi (Ukraine 1905, Israel 1962)

After immigrating to Israel in 1921, he enrolled some years later at the École des Beaux-Arts in Gent, Belgium. During his most active time from 1930 to 1950, he created more than 50 buildings in the International Style, mainly in Tel Aviv and Jerusalem. Together with Ze'ev Rechter, he won the competition for the Mann Auditorium.

Ze'ev Rechter (Ukraine 1899, Israel 1960)

He made Aliyah in 1919 but would later leave the country several times for a longer period to study engineering in Rome and architecture in Paris where he met Le Corbusier. Strongly influenced by Le Corbusier's style, he came back to Tel Aviv and built the Engel House (84 Rothschild Boulevard), the first building on pillars.

Josef Neufeld (Poland 1898, USA 1980)
When he immigrated to the Holy Land in 1920, he had no idea yet that he would become one of the most sought-after international architects of his time. He learned from Erich Mendelsohn in Berlin during the 1920s, came back to Israel, and would finally immigrate to the USA but visited Israel frequently to supervise his projects there.

Genia Averbouch (Russia 1909, Israel 1977)
Her parents made Aliyah when she was 2 years old. She studied architecture at several European universities and opened her own office when she came back to Israel in 1930. She won the architecture contest to redesign Dizengoff Square and became the chief city planner of Tel Aviv from 1940-1945.

Richard Kauffmann (Germany 1887, Israel 1958)
He had already opened his own company in 1914 when he met Arthur Ruppin, the director of the Palestine Authority and co-founder of Tel Aviv who finally inspired him to make Aliyah in 1920. Long before Patrick Geddes, he had developed a plan for the northern expansion of Tel Aviv. This plan did not find any supporters at that time, but Geddes knew this plan and, it seems, took some ideas out of it to complete his own ideas. Kauffmann had already planned the wide north-south connections disregarding land ownership that can be also found in Geddes' plan.

Joseph Berlin (Russia 1900, Israel 1984)
Before he came to Israel in 1921, he had worked in his own business in St. Petersburg. In 1933, his son would join him and together they constructed over 250 buildings until his death in 1984. He was renowned for his use of silicate stone.

The Ring – HaChug
In 1926, Sharon, Rechter and Neufeld founded a circle called "HaChug." They were longing for a new architectural language, a new beginning in architecture. Soon they were joined by Rubin, Karmi, Barkai and others. Young architects, especially those with diplomas from Europe, would join them. Together, they wanted to revolutionize the market.

The magazine, "HaBinyan BaMisrach Karov" (Hebrew for "Construction in the Middle East,") was another of their activities; the first edition was published in 1934, later changing its name to "HaBinyan" (Hebrew for "The Building"). The magazine was a strong supporter of the current zeitgeist: the search for a new identity through having a Jewish state and a Jewish architectural style. With the increasing problems between the Jewish and Arab populations, the eastern style elements on buildings would soon disappear and architects looked for a "Jewish style."

4.3   UNESCO-World Heritage

I N 2003, UNESCO AWARDED Tel Aviv the World Heritage stat*s and recognized the world's biggest coherent ensemble of buildings from the 1930s that were constructed in the International Style. All over Tel Aviv, square-edged houses with round balconies can be found. UNESCO subdivided the city center into zones: A (between Ben-Gurion Boulevard and Bograshov St); B (around Bialik St); and C (upper Rothschild Boulevard and Nahmani St., up to the Mann Auditorium). Together, they form "The White City" with about 4,000 International Style buildings, many still in need of refurbishment today. The municipality made concessions for the refurbishments and allowed the investors to add one or two floors. The original buildings never exceeded three or four floors. The UNESCO-defined zones are home to 2,087 buildings of which 699 are listed. The following buildings are representative of this era. Most of the buildings are very centrally located, others a bit off the beaten path but worth the walk. Even those buildings that are in a deplorable state, still give an idea of the glamour and the spirit of the old times. Stroll through the streets of the White City and breathe the air of nostalgia.

1) 84 Rothschild Boulevard, Engel House (1934). Architect: Ze'ev Rechter

The Engel House is a very prominent representative of the "Modern Movement"; it was the first building on pillars in Tel Aviv, a clear style element from Le Corbusier with whom the architect Ze'ev Rechter had worked during his studies in Paris. When the plots became scarce, the pillar construction was the best compromise to construct as much a possible without neglecting the mandatory green area. The roof garden was a symbol of the workers' movement of the 1930s, a space for encounters with the neighbors. The U-shaped floor plan includes a courtyard to the neighboring Mazeh Street.

2) 33-35 Frishman St., workers' residence (1935). Architect: Arieh Sharon

Arieh Sharon is considered the father of Israeli architecture. He is also the architect of many kibbutzim and made history as David Ben-Gurion's chief planner to build up Israel. This residence is a very interesting and rare combination of residential building and kibbutz. The workers lived in spartan apartments and the mutual activities took place in the basement. As in a kibbutz, there was a mensa and around the courtyard – this building is also u-shaped – the laundry, the kindergarten and the shop for daily supply could be found. Sharon had been a student of the Bauhaus school in Dessau. From his master, the architect Hans Meier, he had adopted the belief that architecture is supposed to improve society.

3) 23 Pinsker St., Mintz & Elenberg House (1935). Architect: Philip (Pinchas) Hütt

This house is also known as the "anchor house" in reference to the overall impression of the façade. The staircase is illuminated by the glass elements, a signature of the International Style. The buildings had been originally planned for single women, with 35 little apartments.

4) 65 Hovevei Zion St., Mirenberg House (1935). Architect: Philip (Pinchas) Hütt

The fusion of two building blocks, as is shown in this construction, is another very typical element of the International Style. Two heavy and independent construction blocks are joined by rounded corners and a shared staircase. The often-found asymmetry is underlined by overhanging wings and integrated balconies.

5) 79 Mazeh St., Recanati House (1935). Architects: Shlomo Liaskovski & Yakov Orenstein

The spectacular façade design acts on the idea of "functional asymmetry": a dynamic façade for a dynamic street and a neutral, calm composition for the quiet side street. The figurative element of the repetition of the balconies plays with the natural antithesis of light and shadow. The Bar Orian architecture firm completely refurbished the building in 2000.

6) 22 HaRakevet St., Citrus House (1935). Architect: Carl Rubin

The *Beit Hadar* as it is known in Hebrew shows the influence Mendelsohn had on his student, Carl Rubin. It was the first building with a steel skeleton in Tel Aviv. Three independent, massive constructions seem monstrous and heavy and still, yet they seem to be floating on top of the floor. This illusion is created by the use of the windows on the entire façade on the first floor. Glass was often used to visually mark a separation, here: the shops and the offices.

**7) 27 Menachem Begin Road, Gavrilovich House (1936).
Architects: Y. Kashdan & E. Shimshoni**
This building is an example of how freely the architects of the
International Style were actually "modeling" their houses. This
unusual concept plays with light and shadow, squares and circles
as well as with concave and convex. The impression of symmetry
and asymmetry is not clear anymore. It seems as if one part of
the building was cut out and put back as balconies.

**8) 29 Idelson St., Max-Liebling-House (1936). Architect: Dov
Karmi**
When Dov Karmi came back from his studies in Belgium, he
would surprise the local market with a new style element:
immersed balconies. In summer, they protect from too much
sun and heat but in winter, they let light and warmth in. The
pillar construction, introduced by Ze'ev Rechter, allowed building without supporting walls and allowed a free planning of the
floor and the façade.

9) Zina Dizengoff Square (1936). Architect: Gina Averbouch
The conceptual design of Kikar Zina Dizengoff – as the square
is correctly called in Hebrew – is the result of a competition like
all the public places and buildings. The winner, Gina Averbouch,
offered the best solution for a mutual design for both the square
and surrounding buildings. The uniform façade design glamor-
ized the square and gave it a harmonious overall picture. In the
original blue print, it was foreseen to elevate the center of the
square and to create parking space. This feature was not realized
and the square became a traffic circle. Decades later, the traffic
on Dizengoff Street became a challenge and in 1978, the decision
was taken to remodel the square with an underpass. This step

diminished a lot the main character of the square. Currently, the municipality is studying the possibility to return to the original blue print. Zina Dizengoff was the mayor's late wife.

10) 14 Ben Ami St. / 8 Beilinson St., Kupat Cholim building (1938). Architect: Joseph Neufeld

The building that is nowadays home to the Kabbalah Center was the first seat of the *Kupat Cholim,* the public health insurance. The original division was based on a functional subdivision of the building with the laboratories and storage in the basement and the offices on the upper floors. The sunken balconies offer shade and perfect ventilation and in winter; when the sun altitude is much lower, light and warmth still enter the rooms.

11) 1 Zamenhoff St., Esther Cinema (1939). Architects: Yehuda & Rafael Magidovitch
The façade design follows exactly the concept suggested by Gina Averbouch for the Dizengoff square. The cinema was built for 1,000 spectators and inaugurated in 1939 with Walt Disney's film, *Snow White and the Seven Dwarfs*. It became a reference for cultural life in Tel Aviv. From 1998 to 2000, the building was thoroughly refurbished and later a boutique hotel moved in. The hotel is reminiscent of the cinematic past of this place: the whole place is decorated with exhibits from the former cinema, not only the lobby, but also the rooms.

4.4   New Building, Old Appearance

TEL AVIV'S REDISCOVERED IDENTITY with the International Style architecture had led to a boom of façade designs in that old style. A growing number of new buildings have been constructed in a design that directly refers to the 1930s. Many times, it is difficult to estimate the period in which a building was constructed. A good example of these new buildings in old appearance is the corner of Tchernichovsky and Dizengoff Street:

12) 69-73 Dizengoff St. / 59 Tchernichovsky St.
In 2001, the architects Ronit and Elisha Rubin built this apartment building with its 23 apartments on 4 floors. Like the Recanati House (79 Mazeh Street), this building has two different façade designs with different characters: a dynamic, "loud" one on the side facing Dizengoff Street and a much sober design toward the calm side street Tchenichovsky.

5
Discover Tel Aviv!

I N 2009, TEL AVIV celebrated its 100th birthday. M*ch has happened since then. The city has increasingly opened up for the growing number of tourists. There are many ways to approach the city: through a city tour, a walk on the beach, following the traces of the Templers and Ottomans or in the shade of great architecture.

City Tour
The sight-seeing tour (bus #100) gives a good general overview of the city. With a convertible bus, you will see Tel Aviv from north to south in 8 languages to choose from. The tour starts in the very north, at the bus terminal of Reading. It is possible to get on the bus at any station. On Friday, the last bus leaves Reading at 14.00. Here are some centrally located stations to start your tour:

1. **Grand Beach Hotel**, vis-à-vis 284, HaYarkon St. (*09.05, 11.05, 13.05, 14.05, 15.05, 16.05)
2. **Hilton Hotel**, vis-à-vis 194, HaYarkon St (*09.10, 11.10, 13.10, 14.10, 15.10, 16.10)
3. **Sheraton Hotel**, 134, HaYarkon St. (*09.15, 11.15, 13.15, 14.15, 15.15, 16.15)
4. **Aladdin Restaurant**, 5, Mifratz Shlomo, Jaffa (*09.26, 11.26, 13.26, 14.26, 15.26, 16.26)
5. **Almaz Shopping Center** 71 Ibn Gvirol/ Rabin Square (*10.16, 12.16, 14.16, 15.16, 16.16, 17.16)
Scheduled Departure Times

You can consult the following link for all stations and their schedules: http://city-tour.co.il//imgs/site/ntext/times.pdf

Guided Walks

The municipality offers free walking tours. The tours are conducted in English; no registration necessary. During the Jewish holidays, there are no tours.

Tel Aviv University: Mondays at 11.00*

This walk is on the university campus and explains the architecture, the sculptures and the historic background.

6. **Meeting point**: Dynanon Bookstore; entrance: Einstein St. / Chaim Levanon St.

* *Except the last week of August.*

Tel Aviv by Night: Tuesdays at 20.00

After dusk, the historical neighborhood of Neve Tzedek and Rothschild Boulevard is suddenly very different from what you have seen during the day: many bars and restaurants come alive. The guides will show you their preferred places and give you interesting background information about the architecture, the people, the nightlife and life in Tel Aviv in general.

7. **Meeting point**: where Rothschild Boulevard meets Herzl St.

Old Jaffa: Wednesdays at 10.00

During this walk, you will explore the famous flea market and go up to St. Peter's Church, pass mosques, street vendors, go over the Zodiac Bridge and discover the small medieval alleys of Jaffa with its artists and galleries.

8. **Meeting point**: Tourist information at 2 Marzuk & Azar St. (near the Clock Tower)

The White City: Saturdays at 11.00
The tour goes up Rothschild Boulevard and explores the side streets. By strolling up the green boulevard, you will learn about the beginnings of Tel Aviv, the architecture, the city's UNESCO status and the city development of then and now.

9. **Meeting point**: 46 Rothschild Boulevard (corner of Shadal St).

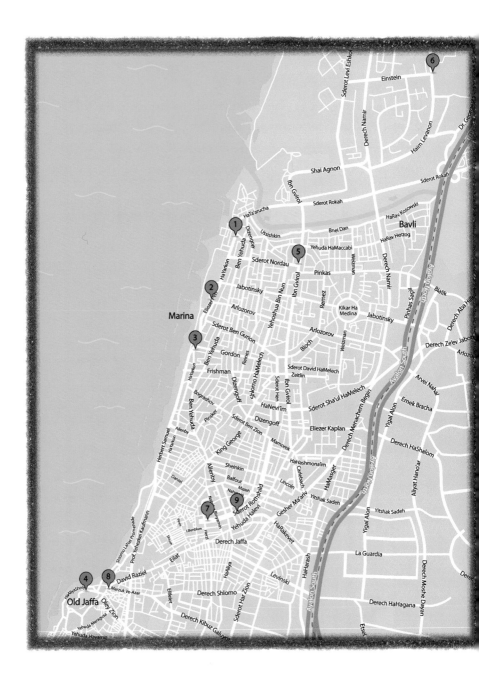

5.1 From Neve Tzedek to Ahuzat Bayit

A T THE END OF the 19th century, Jaffa started to blossom. The already overpopulated medieval town with its narrow alleys was about to collapse. The demand for apartments was very high and the level of hygiene very low. Living in Jaffa would soon turn into a realistic threat to one's health. Under the auspices of Shimon Rokach, Aharon Chelouche (many times transcribed from Hebrew as *Shlush*), Haim Amzaleg and Zera Barnet, a group of 48 families started a new settlement outside Jaffa. They bought land north-west of Jaffa and founded the first Jewish suburb in 1887 – *Neve Tzedek*, Oasis of Justice.

The Neve Tzedek neighborhood with its low-rise buildings and the red roofs has maintained (so far) its village character and most of the buildings are still in the original state. This area is full of galleries, museums, restaurants, cafés, bars and little shops. Coming from Jaffa, Neve Tzedek is on the way to Ahuzat Bayit (original name of Tel Aviv). If you want to follow the chronological city development, it is best to start at the old railway station, HaTachana, with Jaffa in the back. This is how the founders saw it. On the way to the north, you will discover the little side streets where even today there is no side-walk and time seems to stand still, like in Sharabi Street (extension of Lilienblum Street). When you have reached the Eden Cinema, you are standing on the border of Neve Tzedek and Ahuzat Bayit, later re-named Tel Aviv.

1) The old train station – HaTachana
The old train station of Jaffa – HaTachana – is located on the border to Neve Tzedek. The construction of the railway

The Founding Fathers of Neve Tzedek

strengthened Jaffa's position as the economic center of Palestine; in 1892, the first train would run between Jaffa and Jerusalem. In the last years, the station has been thoroughly renovated and stylish boutiques, cafés and restaurants moved into the old buildings. Next door, you find the museum of the Ministry of Defense.

2) Suzanne Dellal Center (6 Yehieli St).
In the core of Neve Tzedek, you find this dance center in a palace-like setting. Founded in 1989, Dellal organizes today over 750 events throughout the year and is renowned for its modern interpretations. The center is home to different dance companies, like the "Batsheba Dance Company" or the "Inbal Dance Theater."

3) Mosaic
A big mosaic has been dedicated to the founding fathers of Neve Tzedek at the exit of the Dellal Center.

4) The Chelouche House (32 Shlush St).
Aharon Chelouche (1829-1920) was one of the founding fathers. He had come from Algeria to Palestine and was an influential member of the society. Last but not least, his knowledge of Arabic came in very handy when buying plots of land. His house on 32 Shlush Street was completed in 1886.

5) Shai Agnon's House (2 Rokach St. / 35 Shlush St).
Nobel Prize winner Shmuel Yosef Agnon (1888-1970) lived in this house from 1909 to 1913. He wrote poetry and short stories in Hebrew and Yiddish in which he portrayed Jewish life in the East-European "Shtetls." In 1966, he had been awarded the Nobel Prize for literature together with the Jewish German writer Nelly Sachs.

6) Amzaleg Haus (22 Shlush St).
This beautiful entrance leads to the house of Haim Amzaleg (1824-1916) who was not only one of the co-founders of Neve Tzedek, but also British vice consul in Jaffa during the reign of the Ottomans (until 1917). As British citizen, Amzaleg could easily circumvent the law that prohibited the sale of land to Jews. As a British diplomat, he signed the purchase of several hectares of land about 15 km south of Jaffa that he would later sign over to Jewish families. Because of this, 17 Jewish families could lay the corner stone of the city of Rishon Le Zion.

7) The Chelouche Bridge
Aharon Chelouche was the builder of this bridge that once crossed the railway and connected Jaffa and Neve Tzedek.

8) Neve Tzedek Tower (65 Eilat St).

The construction of the Neve Tzedek Tower made it finally obvious that the "Oasis of Justice" (as Neve Tzedek is translated from Hebrew) will not be able to preserve its village character forever. Several neighborhood groups have been founded to prevent similar projects in the future. Time will tell if that is possible.

9) Walhalla, the Wagner factory

Right next to the Neve Tzedek Tower, there are two little buildings from the Templers, some of the last remaining from the Walhalla settlement that was established here in 1888. When Jaffa started expanding during the economic boom, the Templers also kept an eye out for new plots. Some of the families settled their houses and garages on the border between Neve Tzedek and Jaffa, close to the railway, like Wilhelm and Georg Wagner who produced water pumps. The Wagner family was one of those Templers who

were allowed to re-open their factories after the end of World War II. The Jews were indignant. After the war, the truth about the Nazis had been known to the world. In 1946, Gotthilf Wagner was murdered on Levanda Street in Tel Aviv. The murder case has never been solved, but a Jewish resistance group had been suspected.

10) The Lorenz Café (57 Eilat St).
The Temple Society of Walhalla had a very lively social life. At #57, there used to be the Lorenz Café. Legend has it that this was a popular venue for the meetings of the Rotary Club and that it was the best place to enjoy a draught beer. The Templers were German patriots and were strongly and increasingly infiltrated by the Nazis who would also gather at the Lorenz since the end of the 1920s. In 1925, the Kessem Cinema started showing movies here. With its location on the Jaffa side of town, it was the only competition to the Eden Cinema that had the only concession for Tel Aviv (see *"Eden Cinema"*).
Since 1970, the building was abandoned. The Schechter Institute for Jewish Culture purchased it in 2011 and completed the renovations in 2012.

11) Former German Consulate (59 Eilat St).
The German Consulate was located right next to the Lorenz until the beginning of World War II. The proximity to the Templers in Walhalla and the Arabs in Jaffa was of strategic importance for the Nazis in Palestine.

12) The Writer's House (21 Shimon Rokach St).
Built in 1887, it used to be the seat of the newspaper, *HaPoel HatZair*. After a successful fight against its demolition, it finally

became a museum. It poses many works from Nachum Gutman (1898-1980) who was also famous for his prose, children's books and illustrations. A big mosaic of his is displayed in the hall of the Shalom Tower.

13) The Rokach House (36 Shimon Rokach St).

Shimon Rokach, one of the founding fathers of Neve Tzedek, built this building in 1887. This house, with its unusual roof, was the first that was finished in the new settlement outside Jaffa. Here, it was his grand-daughter, the sculptor Leah Majaro-Mintz, who prevented it from being torn down. She refurbished the building and opened it later for exhibitions.

14) The Twin Houses (32 Pines St).

Aharon Chelouche built for his two sons, two identical buildings at 30-32, Pines St.; they are called "The Twins."

15) The Eden Cinema (Lilienblum St. / Pines St).

When the Eden Cinema opened in 1914, the neighbors were not amused. They wrote aggressive letters to the municipality claiming that a place of public entertainment would bring the neighborhood down. The operators, Moshe Abarbanel and Mordechai Weiser, had the exclusive license for the local cinema business for the next 15 years. Nevertheless, another movie theater was opened in 1920 on 57 Eilat Street (see 10 above). Since this was right on the border but officially Jaffa, it did not interfere with the exclusive license for Tel Aviv. The Eden Cinema started with silent films. It was the first movie theater in the country and very successful. Later, an open air movie theater was added and the locals distinguished between the summer- and the winter-Eden. The Eden operated until 1974. The building is protected.

House in Neve Tzedek

5.2   From Ahuzat Bayit to Tel Aviv

U NDER THE AUSPICES OF Akiva Aryé Weiss, the society "Ahuzat Bayit" was founded in 1906; a housing company to develop the new settlement the European Zionists were dreaming of. On 11 April 1909, the purchased plots were divided into lots and construction began. In 1910, the name was changed to "Tel Aviv," this was the title Nachum Sokolow had given the Hebrew translation of Herzl's "Altneuland." In the same year, the "Street of the People" – Ha'am Street – was renamed Rothschild Boulevard. Baron Edmond de Rothschild had supported the project financially.

The corner of Herzl Street and Rothschild Boulevard is a good starting point for a discovery walk through the former Ahuzat Bayit; this is where everything had begun. Herzl Street was the first commercial street while the Boulevard was the place where the founders erected their individual villas in the Eclectic Style. This was the main building style in Ahuzat Bayit; a bit of the Near East (many houses had orient-style windows) and some decorative elements from the home country (like little Russian towers). The architecture will change little by little on the way up to the north-east. Take a journey through time from 1909, the year of the groundbreaking, until 1957, when the Friedrich Mann Auditorium was inaugurated.

1) The First Kiosk (Herzl St. / Rothschild Blvd).
The journey starts at the first kiosk of Tel Aviv. Today, you will see a replica there and the main part of the Boulevard is now home to little bars, cafés and tapas bars that operate from similar kiosks.

2) The Weiss House (2 Ahad Ha'am St. / Herzl St).

The house of the Ahuzat Bayit founding father, Aryé Akiva Weiss, was the first in the new settlement. In the following decades, the house would be altered inside and outside. In the 1920s, another floor was added to the originally single-storied house for residential use by the Weiss family. The ground floor was used commercially. Also the façade was changed over the years. The original design wasn't discovered until the whole building was refurbished in the year 2000.

3) Migdal Shalom/Gymnasium Herzliya (9 Ahad Ha'am St).

The Shalom Tower is a controversial office building that can be seen from far away. When it was finished in 1965, it was the highest building in Israel and for a long time in the whole Near East. On 28 July 1909, the cornerstone was laid for the first Hebrew high school in the world– the "Gymnasium Herzliya." Legend has it that architect Joseph Barky had been inspired by the Holy Temple in Jerusalem which led to the Moorish design. In the first years after the founding of the high school in 1906, the students of Yehuda Levi Metman-Cohen (1869-1939) and his wife, Fania, were educated in their private apartment in Jaffa. In 1963, the Gymnasium Herzliya moved to a new building in Jabotinsky Street where today an ornamental iron gate commemorates the school's first building from 1909. The first building had been built on a hill and embodied the values of a new Jewish society: no longer as a house of prayer or the center of daily life, but as a house of culture and education.

On the ground floor and the first floor, there is a public exhibition about the first days of Tel Aviv. Even though the documentation is in Hebrew, the old photographs are well worth seeing. The entrance hall displays mosaics of Israeli artists, Nachum Gutman and David Sharir, which tell the city's history.

4) The First Department Store (16 Herzl St).

Yehuda Magidovitch built here Tel Aviv's first department store in 1925, and the style is very characteristic of the 1920s. On the upper side of the façade, the old name can still be read: "Pensak's Passage."

5) The Shiff House (26 Lilienblum St. / Herzl St).

Olga and Itzhak Frank built this building in 1909, and in those days it was the "Frank House" as it is noted in the archives. Like most buildings of that time, also the Frank House was not higher than one floor and had a red tiled roof. Later, in the 1920s, the Shiff family bought it, modified it like the Weiss House and also added another story. Today, the Shiff House is the private bank museum of Discount Bank which refurbished the building in 2006.

6) Memorial to the Founding Fathers

The memorial at the fountain is dedicated to the first 66 families of the city and was inaugurated in 1951. They had been the initiators who divided the purchased plots among each other on 11 April 1909, and hence led the cornerstone of Tel Aviv. The east side of Aharon Priver's memorial tells the city's history: the planning of the sand dune land, the Rothschild Boulevard and on the upper end, you will discover Dizengoff Square with its surrounding buildings in the International Style. The other side lists the names of the above mentioned 66 families.

7) Independence Hall (16 Rothschild Blvd).

On 5 Iyar 5708 (14 May 1948), David Ben-Gurion proclaimed the State of Israel at Rothschild Boulevard. The first mayor of Tel Aviv, Meir Dizengoff, had left this private building of his to the municipality. Today, it is called "Independence Hall" and hosts the museum of the historic events that led to the foundation of the state. The statue in front of the building shows Meir Dizengoff on his horse.

8) The Golomb House (23 Rothschild Blvd).

This building is from 1913. The owner, Eliyahu Golomb, was the founder of the resistance group, Haganah, and lived here until his death in 1945. At the beginning of the 1960s, the building was taken over by the Ministry of Defense and is today the Haganah Museum.

9) The Lederberg House (29 Rothschild Blvd. / Allenby St).

Like many other buildings from the 1920s, the Lederberg House was also erected in the Eclectic Style. The façade displays ceramics with biblical themes. Downstairs, the legendary "Benedict's" serves one of the best breakfasts in town.

10) Allenby Street

In the days when Tel Aviv was booming, Allenby Street became increasingly important as the new commercial center. According to the city development, Allenby Street would also grow longer. The street starts south of Rothschild Boulevard and drops to the sea right behind the Yemenite Quarter. It gave the residents access to the beach without having to traverse the Arabic neighborhood of Manshiye (today Charles Clore Park).

11) The Great Synagogue (110 Allenby St).

The centers of the new Jewish society were cultural buildings and not synagogues. Hence, the Great Synagogue opened its doors in 1926, a bit off the city's most important street. It is still

Israel's biggest prayer house. The fast and unforeseen growth of the new settlement was disadvantageous for the congregation. Allenby Street would strengthen its position as a commercial center and the residents preferred living in the new residential area that mushroomed in the north. Over there, in the new streets, they would later open little prayer houses. The architect, Aryé Elhanani, was in charge of the building's renovation in 1969 when the new "coat" of pillars was also added. This paid homage to Oscar Niemeyer who had already invented a very similar design in the 1950s for the Ministry of Foreign Affairs in Brasilia.

12) The Palm Tree House (8 Nahalat Binyamin St).

The "Beit HaDekel" was built in 1922 by architect Yehoshua Zvi Tabechnik. During the 1920s, the local architects were searching for a "Hebrew Style," hence, the Star of David on many buildings façades or balcony ornaments. Here, at #8, the menorah is the decorative Jewish element on the upper iron balconies.

13) Bialik Street

This is one of the most interesting streets in the center of Tel Aviv because of its many different building styles. Bialik and its side streets form together the UNESCO-defined Zone C of the World Heritage area. Here, you find the house of poet Haim Nahman Bialik (#22), the Reuben Museum (#14), the first city hall (#26) and last but not least, the Felicja Blumental Music Center (#26) which houses a comprehensive music library and frequently organizes concerts. On the way to Allenby Street, you will find more buildings from the 1930s in the International Style.

14) King Albert Square

At the junction of Nahmani and Melchett – King Albert Square

Rothschild Boulevard

– not only are streets coming together, but also different architecture styles. The Pagoda House from 1924 combines western and eastern elements, like the 21 Moorish arches. The Shafran House on the corner of Melchett and Nahmani is a typical building for the Eclectic Style. Right on the other side of the street, a construction in the International Style shows up.

15) The Levin House (46 Rothschild Blvd. / Shadal St).
Zvi Levin, a Lithuanian-born American, made his life-long dream come true when he immigrated to Palestine after retirement. He appointed Yehuda Magidovitch to build his house on Rothschild Boulevard and in 1924; he moved in and lived there until he died in 1935. The house resembled an Italian summer house with neo-classical elements, a popular style at the end of the 19th century. His family decided to go back to the US and sold the Levin House that later became an English school, then Haganah headquarters and finally it was used as the Russian Embassy. The Embassy left the building in 1953 after a bomb blast. Authorities suspected the attack to be a protest against persecution of Jews in Russia. At some point in the 1980s, the house was sold to Alfred Akirov who refurbished the building completely for which he received a construction permit from the municipality for the office tower behind the building. Until 2006, the Levin House was used by the Sotheby's auction house. Finally, it was sold to the founder of the HESEG Foundation who gives grants to students in Israel.

16) The Engel House (84 Rothschild Blvd).
The Engel House is one of the prominent representatives of the "Modern Movement." It was the first building in Tel Aviv constructed on pillars, an element that reflects Le Corbusier's influence on local architecture. He was mentor to architect Ze'ev

Rechter's. When the building plots became scarce, pillar construction was the sophisticated answer to the question of how to maximize use of space without ignoring the mandatory green areas. The roof garden expressed the values of the workers' movement of the 1930s, a space to socialize for all neighbors. The floor plan revolves around a courtyard that opens to the neighboring Mazeh Street.

17) The Rubinsky House (65 Sheinkin St. / Gilboa St).
With each step, the boulevard is now slowly changing its architecture and the International Style becomes predominant. Lucian Korngold was mentioned many times as the architect of this building but other sources refer to old documents in the archives

that show the names of Markusfeld & Karnovsky.

18) HaBima (HaBima Square)
HaBima is considered Israel's national theater. It was founded in 1913 in Russia and finally settled in 1931 in Tel Aviv. Its own building was finished in 1945 but the company already moved in before the end of construction. From 2007 to 2010, the building was refurbished and expanded. The original building consisted of a cylinder that now has been integrated into the new cube.

19) The Mann Auditorium (1 Huberman St).
The architects Ze'ev Rechter as well as Dov Karmi and their respective teams had both sent their own proposals for the

auditorium and were surely more than surprised when the jury announced that they want a combination of both and prompted them to work together. The project got funding from Fredric R. Mann (1904-1987) from Philadelphia, USA, an international sponsor of art and music projects. The building was completed in 1957 and is since then the home of the Israeli Philharmonic Orchestra. Unlike most public buildings at that time, the Mann Auditorium has no stairs in front of the entrance and seems to absorb the visitors.

5.3   Jaffa – The Bride of the Sea

THE NATURAL HARBOR HAD turned Jaffa already early in history into the economic center of the region and into the focus of many conquerors. Every one of them had left his mark in the city's architecture, like the Ottoman governor (1808-1818) Muhammad Abu-Nabut who constantly constructed new buildings. Jaffa has always been the melting pot of different cultures and religions and this has not changed. Only about 100 years ago, those little streets were crowded and packed with residents and merchants; today, they are picturesque and home to galleries, restaurants and shops. There is not much left from the original Jaffa and its character. The urban alterations already started during the British Mandate. Streets like Mifrats Shlomo and Luis Pasteur were built in those days when the British tore down houses to widen the streets so they could be accessed with military vehicles. Thanks to a group of artists who would settle in Jaffa later in the 1960s and 1970s, at least a part of the town was preserved. Today, the Old Jaffa invites you to romantic walk on its historic streets.

A tour through Jaffa can be well combined with a visit to the Ilana Goor Museum (see **Museums**) or a stroll in the flea market (see **Shopping**), and later you will have the chance to drop by Dr. Shakshuka (3 Beit Eshel St) to try Israel's national dish: shakshuka.

1) The Clock Tower (Yefet St)
The clock tower is legendary. It was built in 1906 by Turkish Sultan Abdul Hamid II who wanted to modernize the country. Fixed hours were considered quite revolutionary in a time when

the day was subdivided into dusk and dawn. The clock tower is the most popular meeting point in Jaffa.

2) Kishle – The Ottoman Prison
The prison of The Old Saray (kishle) was separated from the Saray in 1870 and relocated west of the clock tower. After 1948, it was used as police station until 2006. Currently, there is a hotel project being planned for future use. The relocation of the kishle happened in a time when Jaffa was growing and the city walls were torn down to help the city expand.

3) The New Saray
At the end of the 19th century, the New Saray was completed, vis-à-vis the kishle and the Ottoman administration closed the Old Saray and moved to the new location. The white ruins are a reconstruction of the original neo-classical building that was bombed during the war of independence on 4 January 1948.

4) Sabil Suleiman (Yefet St. at the Clock Tower)
A "sabil" is a public water place either for a ritual washing before the prayers or to refresh after a long journey. Sabil Suleiman was built in 1809 by Suleiman Pasha, the governor of Akko and "boss" of Muhammad Abu-Nabut. It is located at the southern wall of the Mahmoudiya Mosque.

5) House of the Turkish Governor
The building on the right side of the Saray is the former building of the Turkish governor. During recent years, a concept had been developed to turn the building into a Turkish culture center. The works had already started when in 2010 the diplomatic relations between Israel and Turkey tensed and the project had been

adjourned indefinitely due to the Gaza flotilla.

6) The Mahmoudiya Mosque (Roslan St).

The Mahmoudiya Mosque, built in 1812 by Governor Muhammad Abu-Nabbut, is the biggest in the city. Water reservoirs were installed in front of the mosque for the ritual washing. The hidden treasures of the mosque with its courtyards are not accessible for tourists since the mosque is not open for non-Muslim visitors.

7) The Flea Market

A visit to the flea market of Jaffa is a must. The entrance can be easily found; it is the 2nd street on the left coming up from the clock tower, Oley Zion. In the streets around the flea market, young Israeli designers have their boutiques and ateliers. Not only is the flea market a paradise for bargain hunters, there are more second-hand and antique shops in the neighborhood as well as carpet and silver merchants. You will hear full-throated bargaining left and right; welcome to the Near East! Inside the shops it is a bit quieter, but nowhere else in the cities of Europe and Near East are neighbors so close. The whole area around the flea market is a little vibrant world spiced with nice cafés and restaurants.

8) The Old Saray (8-10 Mifrats Shlomo St).

In the 19th century, Muhammad Abu-Nabut expanded the Old Saray that was originally built in 1740. It used to be part of a huge administrative structure that once also included a prison and a public bath house. The Ottomans used the building for about 150 years until they moved into a New Saray in 1890 next to the house of the Turkish governor.

9) The Andromeda Rock

This famous rock is located right next to the port of Old Jaffa and can be spotted from the boardwalk. According to the Greek mythology, Andromeda was the daughter of Egyptian king Cepheus and the Ethiopian queen Cassiopeia. She was tied to the rock to be sacrificed to the sea but was rescued by her future husband, Perseus.

10) St. Peter

The Franciscan church was inaugurated in 1894 after several years of construction. The church is pictorially located on a hill and is the center of attraction for all visitors. The inside is abundantly decorated and the windows are especially worth seeing. It also houses a painting of St. Peter on the roof of Simon the Tanner whose house is located nearby (see 19 below).

11) Jaffa Visitors' Center

You will find the entrance to the underground visitors' center of Jaffa at Kedumim Square in front of St. Peter's Church. The center is located close to an archeological excavation and shows the long history of Jaffa (http://www.oldjaffa.co.il)

12) Gan HaPisga

The park on the hill (*pisga* = peak) with its exotic plants and several sculptures is the work of Avarahm Karavan. The "Statue of Faith" by Daniel Kafri and the "Zodiac Bridge" are popular photo motifs. The view from the top is worth the effort.

13) Zodiac Bridge

The balustrade of this short wooden bridge is decorated with the 12 signs of the zodiac. Put your hand on your sign and make a wish!

14) Statue of Faith (Gan HaPisga)

Israeli artist Daniel Kafri created this four meter high gate-resembling statue in 1977. It shows the three patriarchs Abraham, Isaac and Jacob at different biblical moments: Jacob's dream in which the land is promised to his descendants (left), Abraham's sacrifice of Isaac (right) and the fall of Jericho (top).

15) Ramses II's Gate Garden (Gan Sha'ar Ramses)

On the hill of Gan HaPisga you also find the Gate of Ramses II (1400-1200 BC) that was discovered during an excavation. This gate shows again the rich history of Jaffa and the political interests of the many conquerors who came here.

16) The Al-Bahr Mosque

The oldest mosque of Jaffa looks back on over 400 years of history; the year of construction is unknown but is estimated to be in the middle of the 16th century. Apparently, the mosque was constructed in different stages and the minaret added at a later time. Legend has it that the wives of the fishermen came here to pray for their safe return. After years without usage, the building was refurbished in 1997.

17) Jaffa Port

This harbor is one of the oldest in the world and soaked with history. Pilgrims, crusaders, Jewish immigrants, Arab refugees — they all passed the port of Jaffa as well as countless boxes of Jaffa oranges. In 1936, this port would have to face competition for the first time in its history: the Jews built their own harbor in Tel Aviv close to the Yarkon River. Additionally, a modern harbor opened in 1965 in Ashkelon and Jaffa became still. Even though the big ships stay away from Jaffa, a new vibe has been emerging. Galleries and restaurants have reanimated the old port, fishermen are now selling fresh fish here and yachts are offered for sailing trips.

18) Netiv HaMazalot St.

The street of the signs of the zodiac, Netiv HaMazalot, runs parallel to the port. From here you can walk up to the old city with its narrow little streets. Many of them are named after the signs: Tleh (Aries), Shor (Taurus), Teomim (Gemini), Sartan (Cancer), Aryé (Leo), Betula (Virgo), Moznaim (Libra), Akrab (Scorpio), Keshet (Sagittarius), Gdi (Capricorn), Dli (Aquarius), Dagim (Pisces).

נתיב המזלות

NETIV HAMAZALOT

19) Simon the Tanner (Shimon Habourskai St).
He belongs to the Saints of the Maronite Christian faith and
is mentioned in the Acts of the Apostles (see 9 and 10 above).
According to the Acts, Simon was the landlord of St. Peter. On
his rooftop, Peter had a vision that sent him to Caesarea to meet
Captain Cornelius, a non-Jew. This is the first biblical hint to an
early Christian expansion of the missionary activities outside
the Jewish community. This exegesis is debatable as is the location. This house can best be reached once you pass St. Peter's
at the end of Kedumim Square. It has been in the possession of
the Armenian-Christian family Zakarian for several generations.

20) The Libyan Synagogue (2 Mazal Dagim St).

House #2 is located at the western end of Mazal Dagim Street. When finished in 1749, the building was used as a caravansary and offered accommodation for travelers and their animals. In the Ottoman Empire, these places were much more modest than in other parts of the east; you would even have had to bring your own cutlery and blankets. From 1860 onwards, the building was used by the local population for different purposes. Rabbi Zunana purchased it later to found here a synagogue with a hostel for Jewish pilgrims. The exact year is not known. Years later, the Jews were expelled and were only allowed to pray there when the Arab owner granted them permission. After 1948, the synagogue was given back to the Libyan Jewish congregation. Nowadays, it is only frequented for special events.

21) The Floating Orange (Mazal Aryé St).

At the eastern end of Mazal Aryé Street, after passing the Richter Art Gallery (#24), you will see this exceptional installation: an orange tree floating above the earth. With this work, the artist Ran Morin presents the fusion of nature and technology.

22) St. George (1-5 Louis Pasteur St).

This Greek Orthodox Church from the 19th century is located right on the border with Ajami where Christians from the Near East settled down at the end of the 19th century.

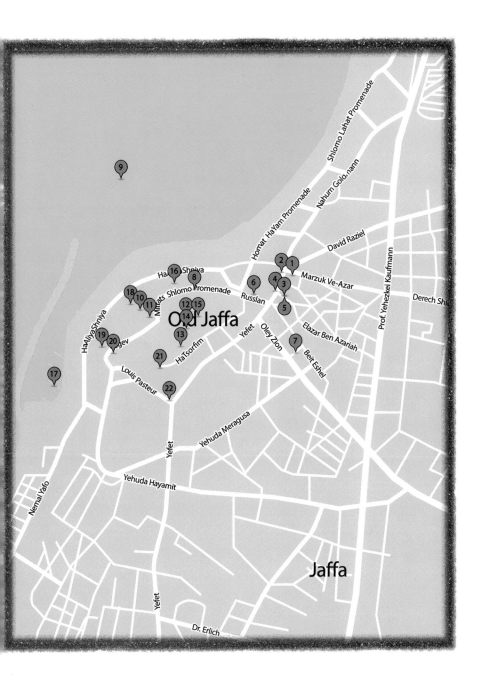

5.4 Ajami

A T THE END OF the 19th century, Jaffa was booming. The economy was strong and there were plans being made for a railway to Jerusalem. It had become crowded in Jaffa, flats were scarce and the expansion of the city became an imperative. Starting in 1870, little by little, the city wall was torn down. The Jews founded Neve Tzedek, the Muslims Manshiye and the Christians went south and settled eventually in Ajami, next to the Muslim neighborhood of al-JabAliyah. On the western side of Yefet Street, the Maronites founded their quarter; on the eastern side, the Copts.

During the War of Independence in 1947-48, most of the Arab citizens of Jaffa left the country and the neighborhood was deserted. With the founding of the State of Israel, Jews got expelled from Arabic states and many found a new home where somebody else had abandoned it. Arabs from other parts of Israel who had not left the country also moved to this area. Over the decades, Ajami got very run-down; the new big beach park, Gan HaMidron, was a dumping place and blocked the view to the sea until recently. The architectonic wealth of the neighborhood was not discovered until the 1980s when investors suddenly had an eye on Ajami and its old villas and palace-like old buildings. New, mainly Jewish neighbors moved in. Since then, the development of the neighborhood has been under fire for its increasing number of luxury condominiums which lead to a further scarcity in affordable flats.

Ajami is located in Jaffa's south. You can discover the Christian neighborhood by entering Ajami in the north and finish at the

Givat Aliyah Beach from where you can walk back to Jaffa next to the seaside. If you are too tired for a walk, you can also take bus No. 37 that stops above the Peres Peace Center. It will take you back to the Jaffa harbor and continue via Jerusalem Boulevard to the Carmel Market in Tel Aviv. The north-bound bus stop is on Valencia Street (becomes Ibn Sina Street) which is parallel to Kedem Street where the bus stop for the southern route is located.

1) Dolphin Street
Fortified by a hearty breakfast at "Abu Hassan Hummus" (at #1) you can now set out on a tour through Ajami. Be there early; once the hummus is sold, the shop closes.

Dolphin Street is part of the Maronite Ajami. You will pass an Italian church (at #11) that is currently not in use and the Maronite church (at #20) which was built by church member Iksander Awad (also known as Alexander Howard) who is buried in the church's court yard.

2) Ytzhak Avineri Street
This street is worth a little detour. In 1855, the Coptic Church founded a monastery here. At the intersection of Avineri and Yefet Street (at #51), you will see the Catholic St. Anthony's church from 1932 and the neighboring Terra Santa High School. In the immediate proximity, you'll find the Anglican Church (48 Yefet St.), also currently not in use.

3) Bathsheba de Rothschild St.
This little side street is hiding at the end the "Scot's House," an old English hospital from the 19th century. In the 1950s, it was closed and later acquired by two Scotsmen who turned it into a hotel. Nowadays, it can be rented for private events.

The Beach of Ajami

4) Sha'arei Nikanoor St. / Ziona Tagger St.

Left and right of Yefet Street, you will discover beautiful old houses. At Ziona Tagger Street No. 6, you see a building that belonged to a rich Arab family. The building style is called "Liwan house." These buildings consist of a big residential area in the middle of the house and various rooms are organized around it. When you cross Yefet Street, make you sure you go by Fakhri Geday's pharmacy at #65. This is a true example of the old Jaffa before 1948. The Geday family has been living in Jaffa for many generations and always owned this place.

5) Dudaim St. / Lotus St.

The streets east of Yefet, Dudaim and Tsonobar Street, are well worth a stroll. Magnificent buildings in different architecture styles are waiting for you.

6) 80 Shivte Yisrael St.

This building is very typical of the Jaffa building style of the 19th century: a palace-like generous and elegant structure with inner balconies and decorated pillars. A "Liwan."

7) 1 Toulouse St.

Architect Yitzhak Rapaport built this modern building in 1935 for a wealthy Arab family who left the country in 1948. With the architect as mediator, they were able to sell the building to the French Republic before leaving. Since then, it is the residence of the French ambassador to Israel.

8) Givat Aliyah Beach

This is the southernmost beach of Tel Aviv. The atmosphere is relaxed and the panorama very different from all the other beaches; to the north there is Jaffa, to the south, Bat Yam. The sea here is rough and the ground rocky; not the best place for a swim, but definitely for a long beach walk. Several good restaurants with Arabic cuisine can be found in proximity to the beach as well as Jaffa Slope Park that connects this beach with the port.

9) Peres Center for Peace (132 Kedem St).

This impressive building is a direct neighbor of the Givat Aliyah Beach. It seems as if it was contemplating the sea. The massive cube is the design of the Italian architects Massimiliano & Doriana Fuksas and was completed in 2009 after 6 years of construction. The NGO in the Peres Peace Center was founded in 1996 by Israel's President Shimon Peres. The organization supports the dialogue between Jews and Arabs and operates in many fields; in nearly all areas of society, the organization offers help and cooperation: medical services, education, technology, economy, etc. The NGO's philosophy is that peace only happens between people and not organizations.

10) Gan HaMidron

This park of approximately 50 hectares is the second biggest of Israel after Yarkon Park and is one of the most comprehensive recycling projects. Nothing seems to remind the visitor of the city's dumping ground that was here until 2010. Today, you see a green oasis next to the sea, ideal for jogging and biking and equipped with nice playgrounds. The park connects Jaffa with the Givat Aliyah beach, the ultimate place for a beach walk.

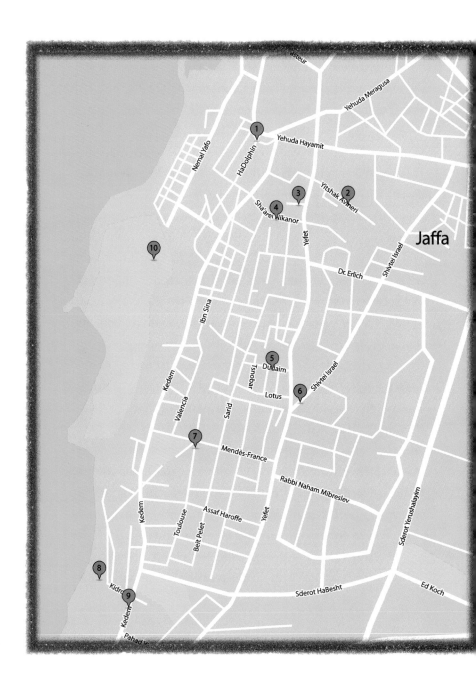

ON THE NIGHT
20th - 21st DEC 1917
THE 157th BRIGADE
52nd (LOWLAND)
CROSSED THIS
FORD & CAPTURED
THE TURKISH
POSITIONS COM-
MANDING IT

5.5 Historic Beach Walk

W ALKING ALONG TEL AVIV'S beaches is also a journey through the city's young history. It is convenient to walk the tayelet (Hebrew for "beach front") from south to north. This way, you follow the 100 years of city history chronologically and avoid sunburn.

1) HaTachana
The old train station of Jaffa, HaTachana, is the perfect start for a walk northward. Only a few years ago, this compound had been refurbished and built up again. It is located in the former district of Manshiye. Jaffa's position as the economic center of Palestine benefited significantly from the railway to Jerusalem. At the end of the 19th century, it started to expand. From 1870 on, the city walls were torn down to support the expansion. North of Jaffa, the new district of Manshiye was founded.

2) The Etzel House
The last survivors of Manshiye are the Etzel Museum across from the old train station, the "Red House" on the compound and last but not least, the Hassan Bek Mosque. After the ruins of Manshiye had been torn down in the 1960s, the plan was to turn this area into Tel Aviv's business district. But things changed, and today the Israeli economy is represented next to the Ayalon highway on the border to Ramat Gan in the east. Between 1947 and 1948, Jews and Arabs competed for dominance in Palestine. At the end of April 1948, the resistance group Irgun (Etzel) conquered Manshiye. The residents of Jaffa could see the explosions from far away. As a sign of victory, the Israeli flag was hoisted on top of the Hassan Bek Mosque. Manshiye was conquered.

3) The Charles Clore Park/ Manshiye

With the new plans for the future city development, the ruins of Manshiye were finally torn down and this district would totally be erased in 1963. In 1974, the Charles Clore Park was inaugurated and modernized in 2007. The name honors the British financier and philanthropist Charles Clore (1904-1979) whose investment group also included the English department store Selfridges. His "Clore Foundation" supports Jewish projects in Great Britain and abroad as well as museums and art collections.

4) The Hassan Bek Mosque

Hasan Bek became the new Ottoman mayor of Jaffa in the summer of 1914. The mosque of Manshiye that was built in 1916 is named after him. Later in history when the aggressions between Jews and Arabs were on the rise, there were repeated sniper attacks on

Jews from the minaret of the mosque. The mosque had not been used for a long time and was finally given back to the Muslim community in 1980s. Today's minaret is double the height of the original which broke down in 1983.

5) Dolphinarium

For the Israeli society, the Dolphinarium remains traumatic. A tragedy happened here on 1 June 2003, when a suicide bomber attacked inside the discotheque. 21 people, mostly teenagers, died in the attack and 132 were injured. In front the Dolphinarium, a memorial stone in Hebrew, Russian and English remembers the victims. On the sign behind the stone, two young people are holding hand and the text says "We will not stop dancing."

6) Border Tel Aviv–Jaffa

During the British Mandate, Daniel Street was the border between Jaffa and Tel Aviv. On 1 May 1921, two Jewish groups violently clashed during Labor Day demonstrations. Both groups were knocking each other around when suddenly an Arab group gathered to beat up the Jews; the violence escalated and led to shootings. The civil population organized themselves and sealed off Tel Aviv. In the following days, they picked up the remaining Jews in Jaffa and cast out Arabs from Jewish neighborhoods. Daniel Street would repeatedly be the venue of conflicts between Jews and Arabs also later in history.

7) 1 Allenby Street/ Knesset Square/ Opera Tower

1 Allenby is an historic address. It used to be the seat of the Knesset (until 1 December 1949) and later of the Israeli National Opera (1958-1982). The construction work for this building started in 1990 and its name is reminiscent of the golden times

of the Israeli Opera and the square in front, reminiscent of the first year after the foundation of the State of Israel: the Opera Tower at Knesset Square. On 19 of 23 floors, there are luxury flats with a private pool on the rooftop. In the lower part of the building, there is a shopping mall with several movie theaters.

8) London Square

Right behind the Orchid Hotel, you will find a little garden with sculptures like ships. This is the memorial for the Aliyah Bet (in Israel, "ha-apala"), the "illegal" immigration of Jewish refugees. Historic photos and documentation explain the events.

On the eve of the *Reichskristallnacht* – night of the broken glass – the government of the British Mandate published the *1939 White Paper* that also contained the quota of Jewish refugees that were

allowed to enter Palestine in the coming years. A subdivision of the HAGANAH, Mossad le Aliyah Bet, organized the clandestine immigration of Jewish refugees from Europe between 1938 and May, 1948. More than half of them were stopped by the British Navy. If they were lucky, they were sent mainly to refugee camps in Cyprus, but other ships were sent back to Europe, a death sentence for the passengers.

9) Dan Hotel

The colorful façade is the curtain behind which hides a true German-Jewish success story: the former "Pension Käthe," a hostel owned by Käthe Danielewicz. Architect Lotte Cohen, originally from Berlin, had built Käthe's hostel here, a renowned accommodation in Tel Aviv with 21 rooms that was later sold to the Federmann brothers in 1947. They kept the name and built up a well-known hotel chain, Dan Hotels, with currently 14 hotel properties. Still today you can find the "KD" on the façade.

10) Abie Nathan (south of the Renaissance Hotel)

Follow the beach walk downstairs, in the direction of the Renaissance Hotel. Shortly before you arrive at the hotel, you will find a little memorial plaque on the wall and a built-in loudspeaker. Abie Nathan (1927-2008) was an Israeli peace activist and founder of the radio station "Voice of Peace." On 28 February 1966, Nathan flew from Israel to Egypt with his own little plane – Shalom One – to present to President Nasser his ideas about peace talks between Israel and Egypt. He got arrested on his arrival and was sent back to Israel where he was arrested again, but later not sentenced. He kept on trying during the years of 1967 and 1968, and each time the Egyptians would send him back to Israel where he ultimately served a short prison sentence. In 1973,

he bought a ship from which he operated the pirate station "Kol Shalom" (Voice of Peace). Outside Israeli waters, he broadcasted pop music and got actively engaged for peace in the Near East. In 1978, he would repeatedly meet up with the PLO for which he also served a prison sentence in Israel. The radio station was very popular but had to close down on 1 October 1993 due to financial difficulties. Abie Nathan received the International Human Rights Award of Nuremberg in 1997. An online radio station has picked up Nathan's idea and created an acoustic memorial for him: http://www.thevoiceofpeace.co.il.

11) Wall Paintings Gordon Pool

Close to Gordon Street, the walls at the beach front are decorated with nice paintings of bathers. This is where the first swimming pool of Tel Aviv had been, the Gordon Pool. The new pool is located a bit further north.

12) Arlozorov Memorial

Across from the entrance of the Carlton Hotel, you will see a green tarnished sculpture in memory of Chaim Arlozorov (1899-1933). The Arlozorovs were Ukrainian Jews who had immigrated to Germany in 1905. Chaim and his parents had lived in Eisenacher Straße in Berlin-Kreuzberg. He had been fascinated by Zionism but until his permanent move to Palestine in 1924, he had been very close to the woman who would later be known as Magda Goebbels (maiden name: Behrend). Once in Palestine, he climbed the social ladder and became the head of the Mapai party and the right hand of Chaim Weitzman. After a dinner with his wife in the Dan Hotel, Arlozorov was shot at the beach of Tel Aviv in June 1933. This murder had never been solved. In recent years, researchers uttered suspicions that the clues could lead to Germany and that this contract murder might have been the revenge of an unfulfilled love (see: "Qui a Tué Arlozoroff" by Tobie Nathan, published so far only in French, ISBN-13: 978-2246751311)

13) Independence Park/ Gan HaAtzmaut

From the hill next to the Hilton Hotel, this little park overlooks the sea. It is a nice spot for a romantic sunset. In 1952, the park was offered to the municipality by a private person. Finally in 2009, the area was refurbished for the 100-year celebration of Tel Aviv. Today, the park is home to several sculptures and a little playground.

The Port of Jaff

14) Tel Aviv Port

A new harbor was another significant step towards independence and construction started on 17 May 1936. Between Haifa and Jaffa, there was no other port until then. The coast was very shallow and big ships came as close as they could, but passengers and goods had to be brought ashore by rowboats. The local economy boomed and at the same time more and more immigrants came from Europe; unloading a ship took longer each time and sometimes the ships would have to wait for days until they got unloaded. By 1949, the municipality decided to expand the port activities and deepened the harbor to allow the ship to land and stop the unloading at sea. Today the port is an attractive place with good restaurants, coffee shops and a buzzing nightlife.

15) The Yarkon Estuary

The Yarkon River presented a natural barrier in the fight between the British and the Ottomans. In the night of 20-21 December 1917, the British troops crossed the river and defeated the enemy by surprise. Because of the flood, the Turks had felt secure on the other side. Close to the lighthouse ruins, a stone column is reminiscent of this event.

16) The Lighthouse

On 13 December 1934, two ships collided in front of the Jaffa port. Soon after this accident, this lighthouse was constructed, starting in January 1935, to improve the situation at the shallow coast.

17) The Reading PowerStation

The red lights of the Reading power plant are very visible at night. For a long time, this was the northern end of Tel Aviv until the expansion beyond the Yarkon River. The newly constructed beachfront of Reading passes the airport of Sadeh Dov.

18) Airport Sadeh Dov

With the intensifying conflict between Arabs and Jews, it became increasingly dangerous for Jews to travel outside the city. The then-mayor of Tel Aviv, Israel Rokach, asked the Mandate government for permission to build Tel Aviv's own airport. Sadeh Dov was finished in 1938 and offered regular flights to Haifa. Today, the airport serves national flights and is also used by the military.

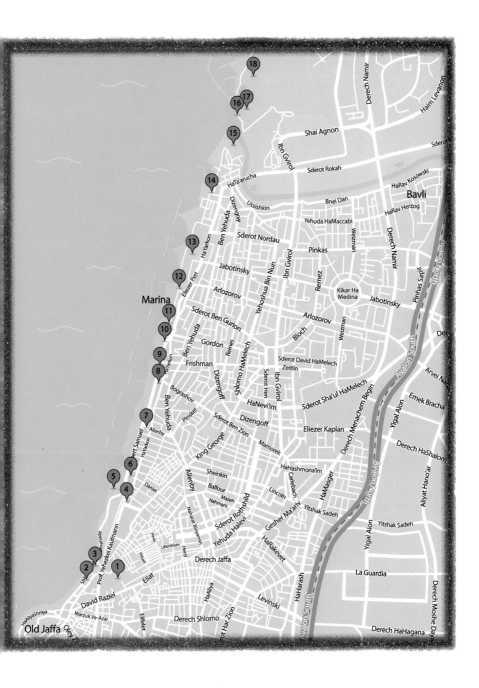

5.6   Further Places of Interest

I F YOU HAVE SOME time left in Tel Aviv, the following places might be of interest to you. They are listed from south to north.

1) American-German Colony
In September 1866, George Jones Adams, the founder of the "Church of the Messiah," and his 156 followers had come from Boston to Jaffa. They bought a plot of land and erected the wooden prefabricated houses they had brought from home. None of them had been prepared for the hardship of agricultural life abroad and only a few months later, in winter 1867, most of them wanted to leave Jaffa and go back home. The majority of them had already left when in the beginning of 1869 some southern German "Templers" arrived and offered to buy their settlement that would later be known as the "(American-) German Colony of Jaffa." Today, there are only two streets left with houses from that time: Bar Hoffman and Auerbach Street. The Templers founded a new settlement east of Jaffa in 1871, Sarona. At the same time, there were plans to open a railway connection from Jaffa to Jerusalem and in 1888 the Templers added another little compound close to the future train station, Walhalla. The railway line was opened in 1892.

2) Beit Immanuel (8 Auerbach St).
During the times of the Templers, the Beit Immanuel was their parish hall. In 1878, they sold it to Baron Plato von Ustinov, the grandfather of actor Peter von Ustinov. He renovated and expanded the building where in 1895 his sister-in-law started operating the luxury Hôtel du Parc. German Emperor Wilhelm

II is also reported to have chosen this hotel when he crossed Jaffa on his way to Jerusalem. The current congregation turned Beit Immanuel into a little historic museum and guest house.

3) Maine Friendship House (10 Auerbach St).

The current owners, Dr. Reed and Jean Holmes, saved the building from being torn down. They opened a little museum that they also show to visitors who knock on their doors outside the official opening hours (Fridays 12.00-15.00, Saturdays 14.00-16.00, http://www.jaffacolony.com, Tel. 03-681-9225)

4) Immanuel Church (15 Bar Hoffman St).

The construction of the church happened thanks to protestant Baron Plato von Ustinov. It was inaugurated in 1904 and after 1948, handed over to the Norwegian Lutheran Church. Several congregations use the church which is open between Tuesdays and Fridays from 10.00 to 14.00. If you are interested in a group tour, the congregation will be happy to hear from you: immanueljaffa@gmail.com .

From here you can take bus No. 40 which stops in front of the Neve Tzedek Tower (other side of the street, direction north-east). It brings you to the HaShalom train station at the Azrieli Center.

5) Azrieli Center (132 Menachem Begin St).

The Azrieli Center is Israel's biggest shopping mall but not the country's highest building. This title goes to the Moshe Aviv Tower in Ramat Gan. However, the Azrieli Center has the highest viewing platform. From the 49th floor, you can see Ashkelon in the south, Hadera in the north and on clear days even Jerusalem in the east. Before going, please check with the calendar on their website since this popular venue is very often booked. On days of reduced opening hours, the entrance fee is reduced as well.

The access to the platform is located on the 3rd floor.

From here, you can walk to the Sarona settlement across the street.

Tel. 03-608-1179
http://mitzpe49.co.il

Sun.–Thu. 09.30 -16.00
Fri. 09.30 - 15.00
Sat. 10.00 – closing times may vary

6) Templer Settlement "Sarona"

During World War II, the British Mandate government had used the site partially for their own purposes and nothing is left from the orchid and orange plantations that once surrounded the settlement. Only the southern part of the settlement is still there, south of Kaplan Street. The Templers had introduced effective agricultural methods with which they managed to harvest large quantities of oranges that were shipped to Europe and elsewhere. Thanks to the Templers, the famous Jaffa oranges became internationally known. The history of the Templers had been forgotten for a long time and new high-rise buildings were already planned when historians suddenly remembered the Templers. In 2011, the renovations of the settlement started. Locally, the area is known as *HaKirya*, the campus. It was the first seat of parliament of the young State of Israel and the area north of Kaplan Street is still in public use.

The French professor Dr. Catherine Weill-Rochant wrote her doctoral thesis about the city development of Tel Aviv ("L'Atlas de Tel Aviv") and literally "stumbled" over something very interesting: the street map of Sarona looks very much like the one of Kirschenhardthof where the Templers had been founded in 1861. Even the street names were in German at that time. The Templers typically divided the settlements by two major streets and located at their junction the community buildings like the school, kindergarten and parish hall.

The complete history of the German Templers in Sarona and the political background can be read in the chapter on urban history of Tel Aviv. If you keep following Kaplan Street westward, you will soon come by an interesting building façade on the right-hand side: at 11 Leonardo da Vinci Street, the city history is summarized in one single painting.

In order to continue further north, take bus No. 26 or 89 at Ibn Gvirol. Right next to the city hall is located the Yitzhak Rabin Memorial.

7) The Yitzhak Rabin Memorial (71 Ibn Gvirol St).

On 4 November 1995, Israel's President Yitzhak Rabin was murdered after a peace rally in front of the Tel Aviv city hall. The murderer, an orthodox Jew, later said he did it to protest against the peace agreement Rabin had signed with PLO leader Yasser Arafat. Right here the memorial was set up: 16 basalt stones from the Golan Heights were lowered into the ground and remind the visitor of an earthquake. This is exactly how the effect of the murder on the Israeli society was described later, an earthquake. On the wall next to the memorial, some graffiti was conserved from the days following the attack when thousands of Israelis mourned Rabin and lit candles. At this time, the square was still named *Kikar Malchey Yisrael*, Kings of Israel Square.

From here, it is only a short walk to the Hechal Yehuda Synagogue.

8) Hechal Yehuda Synagogue (5 Ben Saruq St).

Another name for this synagogue from 1980 is Seashell Synagogue. The construction was financially supported by the Recanati family, originally from Thessaloniki. Greek seashells are supposed to be the origin of inspiration for the building design that aims to commemorate the killing of the Jewish congregation of Thessaloniki during the Holocaust. The entrance is decorated with Jewish ornaments that were cut out of the concrete.

Ben Saruq Street is located east of Ibn Gvirol between Jabotinski and Arolozorov. In immediate proximity, the Gymnasium Herzliya had found a new home (106, Jabotinski St. / Remez St.) after its original building was torn down in the early 1960s to build the Shalom Tower. The Iron Gate at the entrance shows a design that commemorates the original building of the world's first Hebrew High School in Achad Ha'am St.

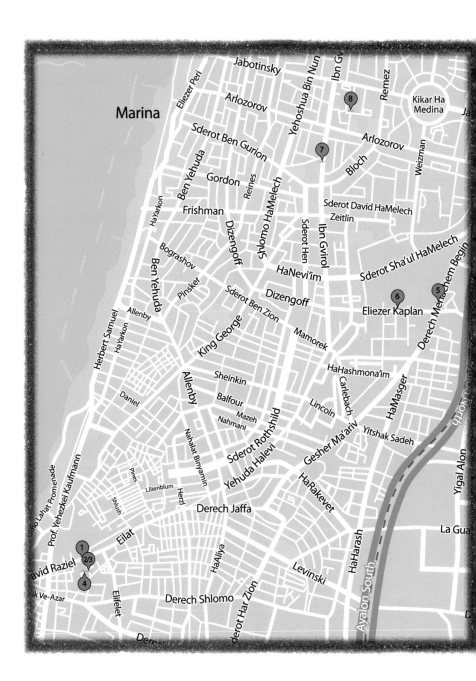

6
Parks

I N AN INTERNATIONAL COMPARISON of urban parks, Tel Aviv
places among the first. The Yarkon Park alone stretches on
3.4 km² while the Berlin Tiergarten comprises "only" 2.1 km².
There are many little green areas and parks throughout the city.
Many people go there to enjoy their lunch, like in Gan Meir (Meir
Garden) close to Dizengoff Square. Patrick Geddes' city planning
had foreseen much space around each building; green areas were
considered essential for the wellbeing of the residents. But when
the city was flooded with refugees from Europe in the 1930, this
concept could not be kept alive. The need for flats was dramatic
and many parks were finally sacrificed. In this context, it is even
more astounding that Tel Aviv is still so green.

1) The **Yarkon Park** (Hebrew: *Ganei Ha Yehoshua* = Yehoshua
Gardens) in the north of the city is the green lung of Tel Aviv.
It contains 3.4 km² of green area and was opened to the public
in 1973. The naming honors Tel Aviv's then-mayor Yehoshua
Rabinovitz. The Yarkon River passes the park and together
with the eucalyptus trees it creates a unique and relaxing atmosphere. The park is full of activities: rowboats (@Agam Park),
playgrounds, bike paths and in summer concerts and opera. It is
ideal to discover the park by bike (see *Transport* for bike rentals).
In the western part of the park, several sport activities are offered
in the "Sportek" center. The climbing wall "Olympus" is located

right next door as well as basketball courts. The park stretches from the Mediterranean in the west to the neighboring city of Ramat Gan in the east and is also the venue of many different events, especially in summer, like opera. Discovering the park by bike is a great way to see all of it (for bike rentals in the north, see the chapter "Transport").

Summer: 09.00–19.00; Winter: 09.00–17.00
Rokach Ave. Park Hayarkon
Tel. 03-642-0541
http://www.parkfun.co.il

2) The **Charles Clore Park** is more of a green area rather than a park. It covers the area between the sea and Neve Tzedek where once there was the Muslim quarter of Manshiye. From here, you have a beautiful view of Jaffa. The park is a very sought after venue for barbeques and provides playgrounds and, of course, beach.

3) **Gan Meir** is named after Tel Aviv's first mayor Meir Dizengoff, a little oasis in the middle of the city. Located between the streets Tchernichovsky and King George, the oldest park of the city (inauguration in 1944) is one of the best places for a little picnic or a breather.

4) **Ramat Gan National Park** (Hebrew: *Ha park ha leumí*) is not part of Tel Aviv as its name indicates, but this modern park of about 2 km² with the little lake and the playgrounds is close to the city and ideal for a weekend picnic after visiting the zoo.

5) After a visit in the Tel Aviv Museum of Art, the nearby **Gan Dubnov** offers a quiet space for a rest. Sometimes, Tai Chi lovers come here to practice.

6) Gan HaAtzmaut (pronounced: *atz-ma-oot*), the Independence Garden, is the ultimate sport for romantic sunsets. From a little hill next to the Hilton Hotel, it offers an unblocked view on the Mediterranean and the beach. Visitors who come early in the morning might discover in the trees wild cats that are recovering from their night out.

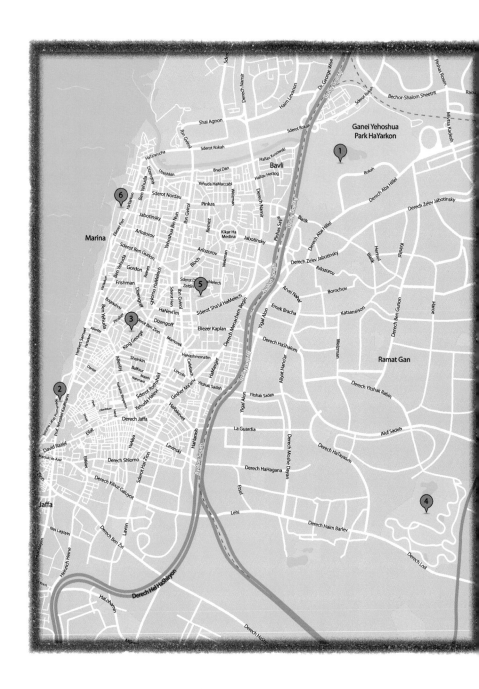

7
Culture

7.1 Museums

TEL AVIV OFFERS A much diversified range of museums and the local art scene, in particular, plays in the same league as those in big cosmopolitan cities. Even though these treasures are hidden behind unimpressive walls, the visitor soon will notice: Tel Aviv is shaking and something is moving! The museums of the neighboring cities bring the offer down to a round figure. This guide only lists the highlights in these other cities, not all the venues. They are only 5-10 km away from the center of Tel Aviv and can be reached by bus or taxi.

! The public and religious museums close on Friday in the early afternoon until Sunday. Museums that are open on Saturday normally close on Sunday.

In this book, the museums are subdivided into the following categories:

- **City History**
  - Tel Aviv History Museum
  - Bauhaus Foundation
  - Shalom Tower
- **Pre-State History**
  - Independence Hall
  - ETZEL Museum
  - HAGANAH Museum
  - LEHI Museum
  - IDF Museum
  - Jabotinsky Institute
  - Palmach Museum
- **Biographies**
  - Ben-Gurion House
  - Bialik Museum
  - Shalom Aleichem Museum
- **Art Museums**
  - Tel Aviv Museum of Art
  - Helena Rubinstein Pavilion for Contemporary Art
  - Ilana Goor Museum
  - Nachum Gutman Museum
  - Rokach House
  - Rubin Museum
- **Religious Museums**
  - Beit Hatefutsot (Diaspora Museum)
  - Bible Museum
  - Israeli History & Culture
  - Eretz Israel Museum
  - Israeli Museum

· **Museums in Ramat Gan**
  · Harry Oppenheimer Diamond Museum
· **Museums in Holon**
  · Museum for Digital Art
  · Children's Museum
  · Cartoon Museum
  · Design Museum

7.1.1 City History

1) **The first city hall** of Tel Aviv is now home to the new museum for urban history, the **Beit HaIr, History of Tel Aviv Museum**, inaugurated in 2009 for the city's 100th birthday. In preparation for Tel Aviv's 100th birthday celebration in 2009, many unique exhibits were collected that were reminiscent of the era before the proclamation of the state. The result is an extraordinary exhibition with old photo collections, films and the office of the first mayor, Meir Dizengoff, and interactive computer installations.

27 Bialik St.

Tel. 03-724-0311

Mon.–Thu. 09.00–17.00

Wed. 09.00-20.00

Fri.–Sat. + holidays 10.00–14.00

Hebrew website: http://www.beithair.org

In the beautiful neighborhood of Bialik Street are located some other museums such as the Bialik Museum, the Reuben Museum and the Bauhaus Foundation. At the southern end, right behind Allenby Street, the Yemenite Quarter and the Carmel Market offer delicious food in a vibrant market atmosphere. The Gan Meir

Park is close by for a picnic. In the park, there is also a branch of the famous Landwer Café where you can have a snack under palm trees.

2) The **Bauhaus Foundation** operates a little private museum that exhibits pieces of furniture and everyday items rather than architecture that reflect the zeitgeist of the Bauhaus School. The building itself was built in 1934 for the Yaffe family and renovated in 1997 by Isaac B. Luxembourg.
21 Bialik St.
Tel. 03-620-4664
Wed. 11.00–17.00
Fri. 10.00–14.00.

3) There is hardly another building that has raised as much public dispute as the **Shalom Tower** (*migdal shalom*). Until 1958, the first Hebrew-speaking high school in the world was located here and the demolition of the historic building has been regretted many times ever since. When the Shalom Tower was inaugurated in 1965, it was Israel's highest building with 39 floors. The photo exhibition in the hall and on the first floor is well worth seeing, even though the texts are mainly in Hebrew, as are the famous mosaic works on the walls that tell the history of the city.
9 Achad Ha'am
Tel.03-510-0337
Sun.–Thu. 08.00–19.00
Fri. 08.00–14.00
http://www.migdalshalom.co.il
>> You are now in the historic epicenter of Tel Aviv. In front of you is Rothschild Blvd. with Neve Tzedek next door. For museum tips, please see "Independence Hall." Depending on the time of

day, you might feel like having a second breakfast at "Benedicts" (29 Rothschild Blvd).

7.1.2 Pre-State History

T HE HISTORIC MUSEUMS IN Israel are rather "political museums"; the country is young (founded in 1948) and its history is inseparably connected to the political events in the Near East. Politics are part of everyday life and if you want to understand Israel, then you might be interested in spending about an hour in the ETZEL museum at the Charles Clore Park (close to beach) where the events of 1947/48 are explicitly explained. The visitor will learn about the background of what still dominates the news today.

4) Independence Hall is the name of the house where Israeli history was made. In this building, David Ben-Gurion proclaimed the State Israel on 5 Iyar 5708 (14 May 1948) only a couple of hours before the British left the country. The museum preserved everything exactly as it was: the same furniture and the same name tags on the reserved seats and many other exhibits that document the birth of the new state.

16 Rothschild Blvd.

Tel. 03-517-3942

Sun.-Thu. 09.00-17.00

Fri. 09.00-14.00.

The *Israeli Defense Forces* (IDF) is in charge of 5 historic museums, of which 4 deal with the Jewish resistance groups ETZEL (also called "Irgun"), LEHI and HAGANAH. The museums are: IDF History Museum, ETZEL Museum, LEHI Museum, HAGANAH Museum and another extra ETZEL Museum that only deals with the War of Independence 1947-48 (at Charles Clore Park). You can get a combined ticket for all those museums that is valid for one monThurs.

! Make sure you bring your passport; access might be denied without it.

5) The **ETZEL Museum** documents the activities of this resistance group who not only fought against the Arab attacks against Jews but also against the British who did not protect the Jews enough against the Arab assaults and would minimize Jewish immigration to Palestine during WWII; Jews were sent back to Europe which, for many, was a death sentence. The main goal of

ETZEL was the establishment of a Jewish State within the territory of the British Mandate according to the Balfour Declaration of 1917.

The museum has two branches: a) 38 King George St. (close to Gan Meir Park and Dizengoff Square,) where the general history of the organization is exhibited, and b) at the beach on the way to Jaffa (Charles Clore Park, close to HaTachana, old train station) where only the events between 1947/48 are displayed in detail.
38 King George St.
Tel. 03-528-4001
Charles Clore Park
Tel. 03-517-7180
Both museums Sun.–Thu. 08.30–16.00.

38 King George St. is also the address of the Jabotinsky Institute.

Ze'ev Jabotinsky was the founder of ETZEL. On King George St., you will find many opportunities to have a bite. Also, the Gan Meir Park is close, where the Landwer Café offers more than a snack on a nice terrace under palm trees. Afterwards, you can continue to Bialik St. to visit more museums (History of Tel Aviv Museum, Reuven Rubin Museum, Bauhaus Foundation, and Bialik Museum).

6) The HAGANAH is the predecessor of the ZAHAL, the Israeli Army. The HAGANAH Museum is located in the house of its founder Eliyahu Golomb and shows the evolution of the organization that initially had been founded for self-defense. In 1909, HaShomer (*the watchman*) was founded after several Arab assaults on Jews during the second Aliyah between 1904 and 1914. From 1929 on, the HAGANAH became the biggest and also technically best-equipped and experienced among the resistance groups. Like ETZEL, they also fought against the British and for more protection of the Palestinian Jews. During WWII, they organized the clandestine immigration of European Jews. Prominent members of the HAGANAH included Yitzhak Rabin, Ariel Sharon and Dr. Ruth Westheimer.

23 Rothschild Blvd.

Tel. 03-560-8624

Sun.–Thu. 08.00–16.00.

On the other side of the boulevard, you find Independence Hall in No. 16

7) The **Lehi Museum – Beit Yair** (Hebrew for "House Stern") is dedicated to Abraham Stern and his resistance group LEHI during the time of the British Mandate (1918-1948). LEHI had split from ETZEL and of all resistance groups, they were the most radical.

The British had been their main enemy and to defeat them, they even considered collaborating with Nazi Germany and ultimately, also to bring the unwanted Jews from Europe to the Holy Land.
8 Stern St.
Tel. 03-682-0288
Sun.–Thu. 09.00–15.00
Fri. 09.00–12.00.
The museum is located in the district of Florentin and the visit can be combined with a stroll through the streets of the spice merchants. (see **Shopping/ Markets**)

8) The IDF History Museum (Israeli Defense Force) is a direct neighbor of the old train station HaTachana between Jaffa and Tel Aviv. The visit leads through 13 little halls and 6 small sites where history of the Israeli Army is documented with military uniforms, weapons, technical developments, files, videos and even a comprehensive tank exhibition.
Tel Aviv Promenade (Tayelet), HaMered St./Yehezkel Kaufman St.
Tel. 03-517-2913
Sun.–Thu. 08.30–16.00.
The museum is located next to the old train station HaTachana and only minutes away from the ETZEL Museum (1947/48) at Charles Clore Park (*see there for more tips*).

9) The Jabotinsky Institute goes far beyond the biography of its founder Ze'ev Jabotinsky. Based on an imaginary conversation, Jabotinsky explains to his son the events happening at that time. The film "Af al pi chen" (Hebrew for *Anyway*) about the clandestine immigration from Europe, the so called Aliyah Bet, is well worth watching.
38 King George St., 1st floor

Tel. 03-528-7320

Sun.–Thu. 08.00–16.00

http://www.jabotinsky.org

The ETZEL museum is located in the same building (*see there for more tips*).

10) The **Palmach Museum** is mentioned here for the sake of completeness. It is open to tourists, but a visit requires prior reservations. The tour takes 90 minutes and audio guides can be obtained in different languages. The Palmach was the Elite division of the HAGANAH and very different from all the other groups. First of all, they temporarily collaborated with the British, and all the members also lived in Kibbutzim where they worked 14 days a month as a way of life.

10 Haim Levanon St.

Tel. 03-643-6393

Sun.+Mon. 09.00-17.00

Tues. 09.00-20.00

Wed. 09.00-14.00

Thu. 09.00-17.00

Fri. 09-12.00

E-Mail: palmach_reservation@mod.gov.il

http://info.palmach.org.il

The museum is close the Yarkon Park on the way to the University. Nearby are also the Yitzhak Rabin Center with the Israeli Museum and the Eretz Israel Museum.

7.1.3 Biographies

S OME MUSEUMS ARE DEDICATED to public figures like Chaim
Bialik, Yitzhak Rabin or David Ben-Gurion. In most cases,
the street is also named after them.

11) The **Ben-Gurion House** is where Israel's first Prime Minister,
David Ben-Gurion and his wife Paula lived. The house and all
furniture and personal belongings are preserved as they were,
including the comprehensive private library. The visitor gains
insight of the public and private life of the politician.
17 Ben-Gurion Boulevard
Tel. 03-522.1010
Sun.–Thu. 08.00–15.00
Mon. 08.00–17.00
Fri. 08.00–13.00.
You can finish a visit to the Ben-Gurion House with a walk to the
Marina where you can have a fantastic ice-cream at "Aldo's." If you
keep walking further east for about 10 minutes, you will reach
the "Tel Aviv Artists' House" (9, Al-Harizi St). that belongs to a
non-profit organization (-> see *Galleries*)

12) Chaim Nachman **Bialik** was one of the most celebrated
among the Israeli poets and renowned for his children books.
Even though the **museum** is almost exclusively in Hebrew (you
can get a folder with English translations of the Hebrew texts at
the entrance), the interior of this villa from 1925 is worth the
visit: a colorful mix of different styles, very typical for its time.
22 Bialik St.
Tel. 03-525-3403

Mon.–Thurs. 09.00–17.00

Wed. 09.00-20.00

Fri. –Sat. + Holidays 10.00–14.00.

Hebrew website: www.beithair.org

The building is a neighbor of the first city hall at the end of Bialik Street, with its History of Tel Aviv Museum as well as the Reuven Rubin Museum and the Bauhaus Foundation (-> see *History of Tel Aviv Museum* for more tips).

13) In the **Shalom Aleichem Museum**, all works of this Yiddish writer can be found, even the non-published. The museum shows all aspects of the author whose regular name was Shlomo Rabinovic.

4 Berkovich St.

Tel. 03-695-6513

Sun.–Thu. 10.00–14.00

Fri. 10.00–13.00 (à *See "Tel Aviv Museum of Art" for more tips*).

7.1.4 Art

T EL AVIV IS RICH in art, whether galleries, art museums or even in the street.

14) The **Tel Aviv Museum of Art** is the primary point of reference for the Israeli art scene. The museum is subdivided into the main house, the Helena Rubinstein Pavilion for Contemporary Art and the spectacular Herta and Paul Amir building that was finished at the end of 2011. In addition to different collections and works of Israeli and international artists, the museum offers a wide range of

activities with special exhibitions, readings, dance performances and films. Among the collections are also the famous "Miniature Rooms" by Helena Rubinstein. The Pavilion for Contemporary Art is not at the same address as the rest of the museum; it is a neighbor of the theater HaBima at the end of Rothschild Blvd.
27 Shaul Hamelech
Tel. 03-607.7000
Mon. Wed. Sat. 10.00–16.00
Tues. Thu. 10.00–22.00, Fri. 10.00–14.00, http://www.tamuseum. com.

Next to the Art Museum, you will find the Gabo Gallery in No. 35 (-> see *Galleries*)

15) The **Helena Rubinstein Pavilion for Contemporary Art** is not only set apart from the rest of the museum, it also has an outstanding personality: it is a platform the Art Museum provides for young artists.

6 Tarsat Blvd.

Tel. 03-528-7196

Mon., Wed., Sat. 10.00–16.00

Tues. Thu. 10.00–22.00

Fri. 10.00–14.00

http://www.tamuseum.com

16) The **Nachum Gutman Museum** is located in the Writer's House that used to be the seat of the newspaper "HaPoel HaZair." The museum shows many of Gutman's works which is not only a collection of extraordinary paintings; he was also famous for his prose, children's books and illustrations. His mosaic works decorate the walls of the hall in the Shalom Tower. The museum also shows works of lesser known names and of Arab Israelis as well who focus on the depiction of the Arab culture in Israeli art.

21 Rokach St.

Tel. 03-516-197,

Sun.–Thu. 10.00–16.00

Fri. 10.00–14.00

Sat. 10.00–15.00

http://www.gutmanmuseum.co.il

17) The **Ilana Goor Museum** is an institution in Jaffa. The artist has spent many years in refurbishing this ruin from the 18th century for private and public use. In Ilana's atelier, no everyday item is safe from being turned into art. The museum shows paintings, sculptures and furniture from Ilana Goor and other artists.

Ilana Goor Museum

The view from the roof terrace is breathtaking.

4 Mazal Dagim St.

Tel. 03-683-7676

Sun.–Fri. 10.00–16.00

Sat. 10.00–18.00

http://www.ilanagoor.com

St. Peter's Church overlooks the sea from the Jaffa hill where you also find the Jaffa Visitor's Center, a little archeological museum below the square. Close to the clock tower, "Dr. Shakshuka" offers a typical Israeli meal.

3 Beit Eshel Street: Shakshuka, except on Shabbat (Friday afternoon until Saturday evening).

18) The **Rokach Haus** was built in 1887 by Shimon Rokach, one of the founding fathers of Neve Tzedek. His house was one the first in the new neighborhood outside Jaffa. The house had been saved from being torn down by Rokach's grand-daughter, the sculptor Leah Majaro-Mintz, then refurbished and finally opened for exhibitions. Even though the documentation in the museum is entirely in Hebrew, the film about the first years of Neve Tzedek can also be seen in English. The historic photo collection is also very interesting, as much as Leah's works and the furniture from the late 19th century.

36 Rokach St.

Tel. 03-516-8042

Sun.–Thu. 10.00–16.00

Fri.–Sat. 10.00–14.00

Hebrew website: http://www.rokach-house.co.il

19) The **Rubin Museum** was the house of artist Reuven Rubin from 1946 until his death in 1974. His work is an example of early

Israeli art: it shows the life in the young city of Tel Aviv and in Palestine before the founding of the State of Israel. The museum presents a permanent exhibition — often complemented with special shows, the original atelier, a room with his private belongings and a reading room. Families and children are very welcome and can participate in the workshops. The museum exhibits online the works of children who were inspired by Reuven Rubin.

14 Bialik St.

Tel. 03-525-5961

Sun.-Fri. 10.00–15.00

Tues. 10.00–20.00

Sat. 11.00–14.00

http://www.rubinmuseum.org.il.

Next door, you will find the Bialik Museums, the History of Tel Aviv Museum and the Bauhaus Foundation.

7.1.5 Religious Museums

20) The **Beit Hatefutsot** (Hebrew for *House of the Diaspora*) is the Museum of the Jewish Diaspora. The history of the last 2,000 years of the Jews outside Israel is told on several floors. The museum is innovative and examines the subject from different angles with additional temporary exhibitions.

Tel Aviv University Campus, Klausner St.; Matatia Gate 2

Tel. 3-745-7808

Sun.-Tues. 10.00–16.00

Wed.-Thurs. 10.00-19.00

Fri. 09.00-13.00

http://www.bh.org.il.

! You can combine the visit to this museum with a free guided walk of the campus that is offered each Monday at 11.00 (see *City Walks*).

On the way back to Tel Aviv, you come by the Yitzhak Rabin Center and the very comprehensive Israeli Museum as well as the Eretz Israel Museum.

21) The small **Bible Museum** can be found in the Independence Hall building and focuses on the role of the printed Bible in the arts. The exhibition show sculptures, paintings, temple models and translations in many – sometimes very rare – languages.
16 Rothschild Blvd.
Tel. 03-517-7760
Sun.*–Fri. 09.30–12.30
*Exception Wed. 16.00–19.00.

7.1.6 Israeli History and Culture

THERE ARE TWO MUSEUMS with a very similar name: the Eretz Israel Museum and the Israeli Museum; they are even on the same street. The first is an open air museum, the other one belongs to the Yitzhak Rabin Center.

22) The **Eretz Israel Museum** is located in the north of Tel Aviv close to Yarkon Park. The museum emphasizes the diversity of the Land of Israel (Eretz Israel): archeology, botany, culture, folklore, modern life, etc. Within the park-like outdoor installation, little pavilions show different aspects. The entrance fee for the planetarium is not included in the museum ticket.

2 Haim Levanon St.

Tel. 03-641-5244

Sun.–Wed. 10.00–16.00

Thurs. 10.00–20.00

Fri.–Sat. 10.00–14.00

http://www.eretzmuseum.org.il.

23) Close to the Eretz Israel Museum, the impressive architecture of the Yitzhak Rabin Center with the **Israeli Museum** inside is difficult to miss; the white roof resembles the Sydney Opera House from far away. This museum deals with modern Israeli society and the development of democracy. It exhibits political events in Israel during the lifetime of Yitzhak Rabin and gives an insight of the private person Yitzhak Rabin behind the prominent politician. The museum belongs to the Yitzhak Rabin Center which was inaugurated in November 2005, 10 years after Rabin was murdered. The center researches the effects the murder had on the Israeli society. Guided tours are available every hour, but reservations are recommended.

14 Haim Levanon St.

Tel. 03-745-3313/3319

Sun., Mon., Wed. 09.00–17.00

Tues.+Thurs. 09.00–19.00

Fri. 09.00–14.00

E-mail: Order1@rabincenter.org.il

http://www.rabincenter.org.il

Yitzhak Rabin Center

7.1.7 Museums in Ramat Gan

R AMAT GAN IS THE eastern neighbor of Tel Aviv. The Diamond
Museum is located just inside the city border.

24) The **Harry Oppenheimer Diamond Museum** is interesting
for all ages. It is located inside the Diamond Center. International
exhibits, videos, multimedia presentations and high-end temporary exhibitions show the visitor the world of the precious
diamonds, about excavation methods, production and deriving
products other than jewelry of which there are also nice pieces
to see.
1 Jabotinsky St.,Ramat Gan
Tel. 03-576-0219
Sun.–Wed. 10.00–16.00
Thurs. 10.00– 18.00
hodm@diamond-museum.co.il

7.1.8 Museums in Holon

H OLON IS LOCATED SOUTH of Tel Aviv and very well connected
by bus. From Rothschild Blvd., it is only 8 km and even a
taxi is not too expensive. Bus No. 3 can be taken at the corner
of Allenby and Rothschild/Lilienblum. If you do not have much
time, you should definitely make sure you do not miss the Design
Museum (4).

1) The **Israeli Center for Digital Art** is an alternative museum

for video, audio and digital art in general. The exhibiting artists come from all over the world, not only Israel.
4 HaAmoraim St. Holon
Tel. 03-556-8792
Tues., Wed. 16.00–20.00
Thurs. 10.00–14.00
Fri., Sat. 10.00–15.00
Bus No. 3 to "Aharonovich/ HaTsionut" in Holon
http://www.digitalartlab.org.il.

2) The **Children's Museum** is a fantastic place for children aged 2-10 and their parents. The website informs about all the activities, but you have to make a reservation to participate because the activities are all moderated events. Currently, there are only activities in Hebrew and English but you should ask about your language (zvia@childrensmuseum.org.il); the museum is very creative and might offer something that suits you. In the past, the museum celebrated a success with the guided tours "Invitation to Silence" and "Dialogue in the Dark" where children learned to understand the world as a deaf or blind person.
1 Mifrats Shlomo St., Holon.
Tel. 03-650-3006
Sat. 10.00–17.00 depending on the activities
Bus No. 3 to "Mifrats Shlomo/Moshe Sharet"
http://www.childrensmuseum.org.il

3) The **Cartoon Museum** is the first of its kind in Israel. The permanent exhibition is as manifold as the events with international artists who take not only Israel but the whole world in their focus of comics to show the visitor the necessity for caricature in society. The event schedule is online.

61 Weizman St., Holon
Tel. 03-652-1849
Mon., Wed., Fri., 10.00–13.00
Tues., Thurs., 17.00–20.00
Sat. 10.00–15.00.
Bus No. 3 to "Weizman/ Eliezer Hoofien" (one stop after Holon
Municipality), http://www.cartoon.org.il

4) The new **Design Museum** is already impressive from the
outside but the admiration continues inside. Constantly changing exhibitions with international artists, monthly special venues
and activities for the whole family (like "Nights in the Museum")
turn the museum into a very special place.
8 Pinhas Eilon St., Holon
Tel. 073-215-1515
Mon.+Wed. 10.00–16.00
Tues.+ Thurs. 10.00–22.00
Fri. 10.00–14.00
Sat. 10.00–18.00.
Bus No. 3 to "Golda Meir/ Kanyion (Shopping Mall)"
http://www.dmh.org.il

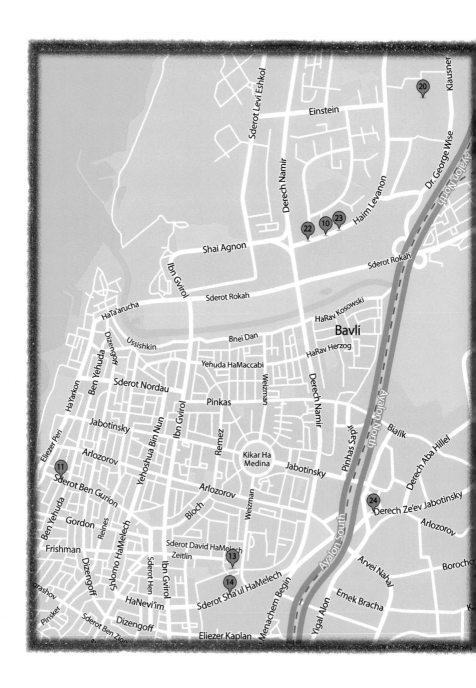

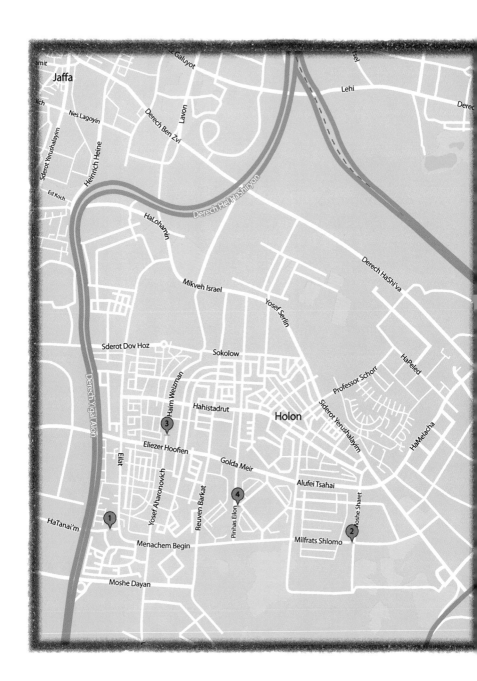

7.2 Galleries

THE ETHNIC AND CULTURAL plurality of Israel is also reflected in the gallery scene. It is impossible to list all galleries – there are probably around 100 in Tel Aviv. This selection contains the most renowned, established, alternative, critical, etc., among them.

1) The **Center for Contemporary Art (CCA)** is by far one of the most creative spaces in Tel Aviv with a huge archive for video art with currently about 3,000 works. The CCA also offers workshops for children as well as extension studies for film artists and curators. A visit to the CCA is an absolute must if you want to get acquainted with the local scene.

5 Kalisher
Tel. 03-510-6111
Mon.–Thurs. 14.00 –19.00
Fri.–Sat. 10.00–14.00
http://cca.org.il

2) The **Litvak Gallery** is one of the most established galleries in Tel Aviv and their artists work in very different mediums: glass, painting, video, etc., but glass is the main medium. No wonder the museum is located in the "Museum Tower," a high-rise glass building. A visit to Litvak is interesting for all audiences whether you want to visit the gallery like a museum or buy a special piece of art. Litvak has been attending collectors for many years.

4 Berkovich St.
Tel. 03-716-3897
Mon.–Wed. 11.00–19.00

Thurs. 11.00-20.00
Fri. 10.00–14.00
http://www.Litvak.com

3) A gentle breeze is going through Israel's leading pop art gallery, **Art Time Israel**. It is a very unique collection; new technology underlines the highlights. The gallery also acts as an agent for sellers. If you are interested in an estimate for your artwork from a Jewish or Israeli artist, you can send a photo by email. The Tel Aviv branch of the Jerusalem-based gallery is represented at two show rooms in the Dan Hotel.
Dan Hotel, 87 HaYarkon
Tel. 03-529.3548
Sun.–Thu. 10.00–19.00
Fri. 10.00–13.30
http://www.art-time.co.il

4) Dvir is THE reference for established Israeli and international artists and those who are about to consolidate their career. Dvir shows independent exhibitions in three different locations. http://www.dvirgallery.com.
A) 11 Nahum HaNavi St.
Tel. 03-604-3003 Tues.–Thurs. 11.00–18.00
Fri., Sat. 10.00–13.00.
B) 11 Nitzana St.
Tel. 03-683-2345 (please consult website above for opening hours)

5) Since its founding in Neve Tzedek in 1985, the **Chelouche Gallery** has exhibited works from local and international artists and is today renowned for contemporary art. The works are extensive and of diverse characters and forms: sculptures, video art,

paintings, installations, etc. In October 2010, the gallery moved to Mazeh Street, a spectacular building by Josef Berliner, the so-called "Twin House." It was the first of its kind and was supposed to be the home of the architect and his brother, but later, the Association of Architects and Engineers and the Academy for Architecture moved in.

7 Mazeh St.

Tel. 03-620-0068

Mon.–Thurs. 11.00–19.00

Fri. 10.00–14.00

Sat. 11.00–14.00

http://www.chelouchegallery.com

6) The **Kayma** gallery is located in a refurbished Ottoman building. The name "kayma" is derived from the Aramaic word for

"survival." This is the main topic: sustainability in contemporary art. Kayma focuses on experimental recycling techniques.
26 Ben Dosa
Tel. 03-518-5144
Tues.–Thurs. 11.00–14.00 and 16.00–19.00
Fri.+Sat. 11.00–14.00
http://www.kayma.net
The Jaffa flea market is only a short walk away.

7) The **Hezi Cohen Gallery** can be considered the "free spirit" among the galleries; where else in this country would it be possible to get in touch with an Iranian artist? In 2011, Iranian artist Mitra Tabrizian exhibited his work, "tension." Hezi Cohen wants to show the artworks in their self-defined nature and provides an exhibition space of 450 m² on two levels that individually adapt to the exhibits.
54 Wolfson St.
Tel. 03-639-8788
Sun.–Thu. 10.30–19.00
Fri. 10.00–14.00
Sat. 11.00–14.00
http://www.hezicohengallery.com

8) The **Alfred Gallery** was founded in 2005 by a group of artists and is a true non-profit organization. Their aim is to give the not-yet-established a chance to exhibit their work. The exhibits are each of very different kinds (paintings, sculptures, photos, etc) and are very often rotated with new ones.
19 Ben Atar
Tel. 052-801-4848
Mon.–Thurs. 17.00–21.00

Fri. 10.00–14.00
Sat. 11.00-15.00
http://alfredgallery.com

9) Nomen est omen, **Florentin 45** is located right here. The gallery is very dynamic and shows all the time new exhibits of modern Israeli art, much of it comes from the best ateliers Israel has to offer.
45 Florentin
Tel. 050-276-3249
Mon.–Sat. 11.00–13.00
Mon.–Thurs. 16.00–18.00
http://www.florentin45.com

10) Gebo Art Space offers local artists the opportunity to exhibit their works. The exhibitions show modern Israeli art and change often.
35 Shaul HaMelech, America House
Tel. 03-695-2268
Mon.–Thurs. 11.00–19.00
http://www.gebogallery.com

11) The **Tel Aviv Artists House** belongs to the association of artists and sculptors, a non-commercial organization that takes care of the social needs of artists and dates back to 1934. With its manifold program of activities as well as monthly new exhibitions, this place is an important player in the local art scene.
9 Al-Harizi St.
Tel. 03-524-6685
Mon.–Thurs. 10.00–13.00 17.00–19.00
Fri. 10.00–13.00

Sat. 11.00–14.00

http://www.artisthouse.co.il

12) P8 Art Gallery Some galleries are a bit more alternative than the others and their relationship with art is a bit different, like the P8 Art Gallery where it's mainly the works of the five founders that are presented, but they also invite others to their space.

8 Poriya

Tel. 050-861-6001

Wed.+Thurs. 16.00–19.00

Fri.+Sat. 11.00–14.00

http://www.p8gallery.net.

13) Kibbutz, The Gallery focuses on Israeli culture in art. The works reflect the topics of Israeli society and is connected to 15 other galleries in the kibbutzim.

25 Dov Hoz

Tel. 03-523-2533

Mon.–Thurs. 11.00–15.00, 16.00–18.00

Fri. 11.00–14.00

http://www.kibbutzgallery.org.il

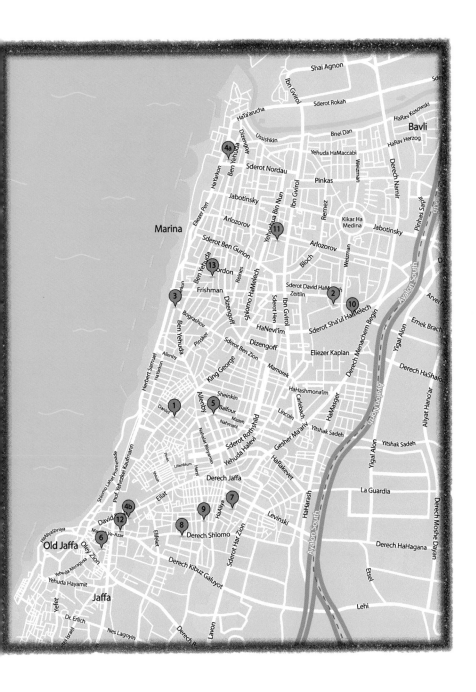

TAPAC, Tel Aviv Performing Art Center

7.3 Theaters and Concert Halls

T EL AVIV HAS MUCH to offer, even for those who do not speak
Hebrew because many performances come with English
supertitles, e.g., at the opera. Ballet and contemporary dance
are very much worth the visit as well; often these are Israeli productions.

7.3.1 Opera and Theater

1) The Opera
Tel Aviv is proud of its opera tradition which dates back to the
1920. Jewish-Russian composer Mordechai Golinkin dedicated
his life to the creation of an opera for the Land of Israel. He
most probably could have not imagined how much the Israelis
would still love opera in the 21st century when he published his
thesis, "The Vision of the Hebrew Art Temple of Opera Work in
Palestine" in 1917.
Golinkin immigrated in 1923. On 28 July 1923, the "Palestine
Opera" was born with the performance of Verdi's "La Traviata."
On the way to today's "New Israeli Opera," mainly financial difficulties put the project at risk more than once, but political
turbulence also put obstacles along the way. Legend has it that
the British Mandate government had asked Golinkin to not show
the opera "La Juive" (the Jewess) from HaLevy. The performance
had already been very successful in Tel Aviv and was supposed
to be shown in Jerusalem, but the British feared problems with
the non-Jewish population here: Christians. Golinkin agreed but

did not stop the project; he simply changed the title to "Rachel" which was the name of the main figure and performed the opera as scheduled. There are no reports about any negative reactions from the Christians.

Golinkin managed his opera house until 1927 when he left for the US to raise funds. Later, in 1940, George Singer and Riga-born Marc Lavry founded the "Palestine Folk Opera." Lavry had been the manager of the Berlin Symphony Orchestra between 1929 and 1932, and in the following two years, the opera in Riga. In 1935, he fled to Israel. His opera production "Dan HaShomer" (*Dan the Watchman*) was shown in Tel Aviv in 1945. It was the first opera production in the country and was based on a play from Shin Shalom. It became Lavry's very own signature to reflect political events in his work, especially topics referring to the European presence in the Near East and the conflicts with the Arab population.

Edis De Philippe (*1912, New York) is another name that is deeply connected with the Israeli opera culture. Singer de Philippe successfully convinced the Zionist Union in Basel that Tel Aviv needed a permanent and locally based opera. From 1947 until her death in 1979, she directed the "National Israeli Opera." Under her auspices, many Israeli but also international singers started their careers, like Plácido Domingo who studied here in the 1960s. Until 1958, de Philippe was renting space from local theaters and would then move to

1 Allenby Street, the former seat of parliament. In the early years, de Philippe funded the opera house with her own money, but in 1982, it was finally closed due to lack of funding; neither the state nor the municipality was willing to give more grants. De Philippe had been a controversial figure; many would even call her management a dictatorship. She had dedicated her life to

the Israeli opera culture and thanks to her; the citizens of Tel Aviv never lost their enthusiasm for it. It is no wonder that in the years following the closure, they would express their displeasure about this loss.

Finally, the **New Israeli Opera** was founded. It is a joint-venture between the Cameri Theater and the Israeli Chamber Orchestra which is located in the Tel Aviv Performing Art Center (TAPAC) with 1,500 seats since 1994. The operas are sung in the original language with Hebrew and English supertitles.

Guided visits (only with reservations):
- Groups can book a "Backstage Tour" which shows you the world behind the curtains. Duration: 90 minutes. Languages: English and Hebrew. Tel. 03-692-7863.
- Single tourists might be interested in another visit: 75 minutes before the performance, you can observe the preparations and watch the artists getting ready. Tel. 03-692-7777. Price: 25 NIS.

Tel Aviv Performing Arts Center
19 Shaul Ha Melech Blvd.
Box office: kupa@tapac.org.il
Tel. **03-692-7777**
http://www.israel-opera.co.il.

2) Every year, more than 900,000 visitors come to the **Cameri Theater** in the TAPAC. Since its founding in 1944, it is an inherent part of Israeli culture. The Cameri wants to give more than a good performance; it wants to bring the theater to everybody. It is a theater with social responsibility: translations into different languages, special tariffs, barrier-free, etc. Three times a week,

the Cameri plays with English supertitles: "See it in Hebrew read it in English."
Tel Aviv Performing Arts Center
19 Shaul Ha Melech Blvd.
Tel. 03-606-1960 or 03-606-0900
Email: booking@cameri.co.il
Hebrew website: http://www.cameri.co.il

3) HaBima is Israel's national theater. It was founded already in 1913 in Russia and had always struggled with anti-Semitic hostility until the 1920s when the group decided to split during a concert tour in the United States. HaBima started again in 1931 in Tel Aviv and moved into its own theater house in 1945 even before the construction was finished. Since HaBima had been awarded the Israel Prize (that acknowledges engagement for Israeli society) in 1958, the Israelis call it THE Israeli theater house. It is the only member of the European Theater Union (UTE) outside Europe and performs around the globe. Information on performances in English: on request.
Kikar HaBima
Tel. 03-629-5555
E-mail: sherut@habima.org.il
http://www.habima.co.il.

4) The Yiddish Theatre in Israel is one of the most charming among all theaters. As the name already indicates, they play in Yiddish. Headphones with simultaneous translations are pro-vided only in Hebrew and Russian. The company published some examples of its repertoire on YouTube. This way, you can test whether you understand the Yiddish language. The actors are fabulous. They show Jewish culture from many angles, whether

traditional, eastern European or modern productions, the Yiddish Theatre hits the mark. The group performs all over the country; in Tel Aviv they play (most of the time) in the house of the Zionist Organization of America – ZOA, but check your tickets! (4a) 26, Ibn Gvirol, @ ZOA. The box office is located here:
28 Bialik St.
Tel. 03-525-4660
 Sun. Mon. Wed. Thurs. 09.00-20.00
Tues. 09-00-16.00
http://www.yiddishpiel.co.il
http://www.youtube.com/user/yiddishpiel

5) A visit to the **Na Laga'at Center** in Jaffa port is a very enriching experience. While Israeli shops often put little signs on their goods with "na lo laga'at" ("please do not touch,") here, we are in a "please touch" space. Blind and deaf actors present an impressive show with English supertitles on Sunday, Tuesday and Thursday at 20.30 (subject to change!) In the center, there is also the Kapish Café and the Black Out Restaurant, a dark restaurant with blind waiters.
HaAliyah HaShniya, Jaffa Port
Tel. 03-633-0808
http://www.nalagaat.org.il
http://www.youtube.com/user/nalagaat

6) **Mayumana** is an international creative group that communicates with the audience in its very own way. The participants are actors, musicians, dancers, acrobats in one. Lots of rhythm and visual effects flow from the stage into the audience. Founded by three Israelis, Mayumana has become so successful that they decided to have two groups: one performs in Tel Aviv and another

one is always on tour.

Mayumana House

Tel. 03-521-5200

15 Louis Pasteur St.

http://www.Mayumana.com

http://www.youtube.com/user/mayumanamomentum

7) The **Clipa Theater**, founded in 1995, is considered Israel's best "visual theater." Idit Herman and Dmitry Tyulpanov have founded a company that combines contemporary dance and musical effects in a new way and with self-designed costumes.

38 HaRakevet St.

Tel. 03-687-9219

E-mail: clipa@netvision.co.il

http://www.clipa.co.il

http://www.youtube.com/user/clipatheater

7.3.2 Classical Music

8) The **Israeli Philharmonic Orchestra** (IPO), originally "The Palestine Symphony," is world-renowned and looks back on 75 years of history. On 26 December 1936, the IPO gave its first concert directed by conductor Arturo Toscanini on the fairgrounds in the north of Tel Aviv. Prior to this, the Polish violinist Bronisław Huberman (1882–1947) had convinced 75 Jewish colleagues from different European countries to immigrate to Palestine to found a new orchestra. Huberman saw no future for Jewish musicians in fascist Europe where more and more of them were harassed and became jobless. In the first two years,

the orchestra would still play many works from Richard Wagner, a known anti-Semite, but since the "Night of the Broken Glass" ("Reichskristallnacht") of 9 November 1938, the orchestra adheres to its ban of Wagner compositions. 1936 was also the year of birth of the Indian conductor Zubin Mehta who was appointed music director for life of the orchestra. Since 1968, he had already been their advisor. Leonard Bernstein (1918-1990) was another big name that collaborated with the orchestra since 1948, and who in 1988 became awarded with the title of "conductor of honor" of the orchestra. Bernstein and Mehta are, of course, extraordinary musicians, but there is one other reason why the Israelis love them dearly: both never left the country during wars. They organized concerts at war places to morally support the population and the soldiers. Since 1957, the Frederic R. Mann Auditorium at the upper end of Rothschild Boulevard is the permanent home of the orchestra, right next to HaBima Theater. The building was financially supported from the American philanthropist Frederic R. Mann (1904-1987) from Philadelphia, an international promoter of art and music projects.

Frederic R. Mann Auditorium

1 Huberman St.

Tel. 03-621-1777

http://www.ipo.co.il

http://www.youtube.com/user/IPOvideos

9) Together with the IPO, the **Israeli Chamber Orchestra** (ICO) belongs to the most renowned in Israel. It was founded in 1965 by Gary Bertini, an Israeli conductor and composer. The ICO plays music from Israeli and international composers, contemporary as well as baroque. The participation of the ICO at the Wagner festivals in Bayreuth, Germany, in 2011 was discussed

very controversially. They were the first Israeli orchestra to play Wagner, unlike the IPO which refused to play Wagner since 1938.
Israel Chamber Orchestra
10 She'erit Israel St.
Tel. 03-518.8845
Tel. Tickets 03-518.8845/6
E-mail: info@ico.co.il
http://www.ico.co.il

10) The youngest of the local orchestras is the **Israeli Contemporary Players** (ICP). Founded in 1991, the orchestra plays mainly music from the 20th century, often from Israeli composers. The ICP often plays outside Israel, but its home is in Jaffa.
Club Hateiva
19 Sderot Yerushalayim
Tel. 03-682-2403
http://www.ensemble21.org.il

11) The **Felicja Blumental Music Center** is home to an extensive music library since 1951 and frequently organizes concerts, workshops and further education. The house is idyllically located next to Tel Aviv's first city hall at the end of Bialik St. In 1991, the center was named after Polish born pianist Felicja Blumental (1908-1991). Since 1999, the Felicja Blumental Festival

takes place every year (April/ May), organized from the Tel Aviv Museum of Art. Every day, there are up to 5 events filled with theater plays, music and films in different venues in the city.
26 Bialik St.
Tel. 03-620-1185
Office Sun.+Tues. 09.00–13:45
Mon., Wed., Thurs. 12.00–18.45
http://www.fbmc.co.il
http://www.blumentalfestival.com

12) Tzavta is a little theater that also offers classical concerts every Saturday at 11.00
Ibn Gvirol St.
Tel. 03-695-0156/7
Opening hours of the box office:
Sun.–Thu. 10.00–16.00 and 19.00–20.30
Fri. 10.00–14.00 and 19.00–01.00
Sat. 10.00–11.30 and 19.00–21.00
E-mail: mali-dor@inter.net.il
Hebrew website: http://www.tzavta.co.il

13) The Tel Aviv Museum of Art (TA Museum) houses the **Recanati Hall**. Handpicked concert series, contemporary art performances and a high-quality standard turn the hall into a very sought after venue.
27 Shaul Hamelech Blvd.
Tel. 03-607-7009
music@tamuseum.com
http://www.tamuseum.com/music-lobby
http://www.youtube.com/user/musictamuseum

7.3.3 Dance

14) The **Suzanne Dellal Center** is all about dance: education, training, workshops, festivals. Founded in 1989, the center is situated in a palace-like residence in the heart of Neve Tzedek and shows more than 750 events every year. Three stages and the box office are located at the site. Pre-purchased tickets can be returned up to 48 hours before the performance and a full refund will be issued.

5 Yechieli St.

Box office: Tel. 03-510-5656

Tel. 03-510-5657

E-mail: info@suzannedellal. org.il

Sun.–Thu. 09.00–19.00

Fri. and before holidays 09.00–13.00.

Same-day ticket sales open 2 hours before the start of an event. http://www.suzanne-dellal.org.il

http://www.youtube.com/ user/suzannedellalcentre.

7.3.4 Culture – Miscellaneous

15) The **ENAV** cultural center shows performances of different types: art, dance, music, theater. Since the ENAV did not have its own website when this book was printed and publishes mostly information in Hebrew, it is recommendable to just go by and have a look what is scheduled for the upcoming days. It is situated on the top floor of the shopping center next to the municipality and the Rabin Memorial.

71 Ibn Gvirol, Tel. 03.521.7760.

Foreign Cultural Representations

Many foreign institutions offer a very interesting cultural program and are very open to tourists and non-Hebrew speakers. Please consult their websites for further information.

16) Goethe Institut

Asia House

4 Weizman St.

Tel. 03-606-0500

E-mail:info@telaviv.goethe.org

http://www.goethe.de/telaviv (German, Hebrew).

17) Instytut Polski

Asia House

4 Weizman St.

Tel. 03-696-2053/9

Email: telaviv@instytutpolski.org

http://www.polishinstitute.org.il (Polish, English, Hebrew).

18) Czech Centre Tel Aviv

23 Zeitlin St.

Tel. 03-691-1216

E-mail: cctelaviv@czech.cz,

http://tel-aviv.czechcentres.cz (Czech, English).

19) Romanian Culture Institute Tel Aviv
8 Shaul Ha Melech
Tel. 03-696-1746
E-mail:office@icrtelaviv.org,
http://www.icr.ro/tel-aviv (Romanian, English, Hebrew).

20) Instituto Cervantes Tel Aviv
7 Shulamit St.
Tel. 03-527-9992
E-mail: centel@cervantes.es,
http://telaviv.cervantes.es (Spanish, Hebrew).

21) L'Institut Français
7 Rothschild Blvd.
Tel. 03-796-8000
E-mail: accueilifta@ambfr-il.org
http://www.ambafrance-il.org/-LA-CULTURE-.html (French, Hebrew).

22) Instituto Italiano di Cultura
25 HaMered
Tel. 03-516-1361
E-mail: iictelaviv@esteri.it
http://www.iictelaviv.esteri.it/IIC_Telaviv (Italian, Hebrew).

7.3.5 Box Offices

23) Hadran, 90, Ibn Gvirol St., Tel. 03-521.5200.
24) Castel, 153, Ibn Gvirol St., Tel. 03-604.5000.
25) Le'an, 101, Dizengoff St., Tel. 03-524.7373.

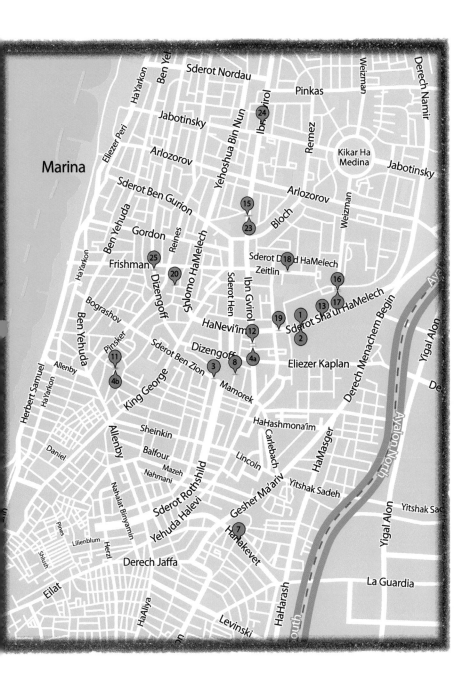

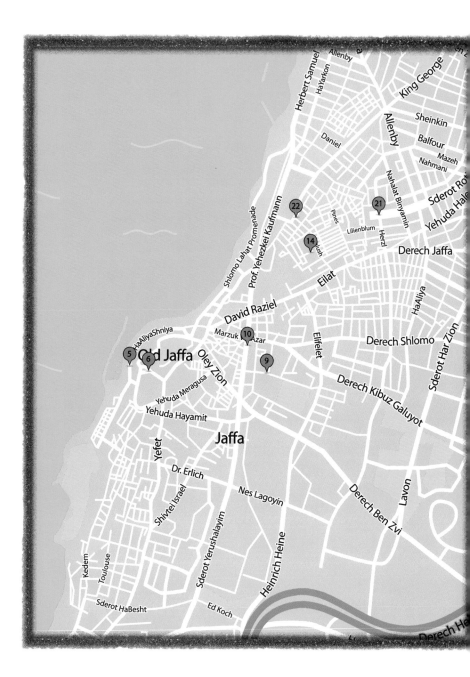

8
Children

I SRAELIS LOVE CHILDREN AND it is very easy to travel in this
country with young family members. Everybody is open and
helpful towards their needs, whether you are asking for special
food or to set out your baby's accessories in the washroom. The
following places specialize in entertainment for children of different ages.

8.1 Museums

T HE FOLLOWING MUSEUMS FREQUENTLY offer activities for
children (see *Museums*):
· Reuven Rubin Museum
· Eretz Israel Museum
· Children's Museum (Holon)

8.2 Parks

T HE PARKS LISTED BELOW are great for a visit with children
(see *Parks*):
· Yarkon Park (with Zapari and Luna Park)

- Ramat Gan National Park (in Ramat Gan, next to the zoo)
- Charles Clore Park (at the beach)

1) The birds park **Zapari** gives children and their parents the opportunity to watch beautiful creatures and you can also participate in the feeding. But there is more on the compound: a children's zoo, tropical plants, waterfalls... as well as the adventure playground "Junga Junga." The park is located in the north of Tel Aviv.

Yarkon Park (Hebrew: *Ganei HaYehoshua*)

Open every day from 10.00 - 15.00 and 17.00, depending on the time of year.

The children's zoo and the adventure playground are only open on Shabbat.

The park is easy to reach by train. The entrance is located within walking distance south of the university train station.

Bus No. 25 (to university) also stops nearby. Sderot Rokach

Tel. 03-642-2888

http://www.zapari.co.il

49 Theme Parks

2) **Superland** is a modern theme park and offers entertainment for the whole family. It is located south of Tel Aviv between Bat Yam and Rishon Le Zion and the sea.

Sderot Maryland, Rishon Le Zion

Tel. 03-961-9065

Only open on Shabbat and holidays (10.00-21.00).

http://www.superland.co.il

3) While Superland is more for adults and older children, **Luna Park** offers entertainment for the younger family members: roller

coasters, bumper cars, and merry-go-rounds like "back then." Luna Park can be found next to Zapari at Yarkon Park in the north of Tel Aviv.

It can be reached by train (university station) and bus (e.g., No. 25 to university). In July and August, the park is open daily, in other months only on Shabbat and holidays (10.00-21.00).

Sderot Rokach

Tel. 03-642-7080

http://www.lunapark.co.il

4) Another neighbor of Luna Park and Zipari is the water park **Maimadion** (Hebrew *maim* = water), a great place to be in the hot summer: like a little oasis, this place offers shade, green areas, water slides and swimming pools in all varieties. The entrance is exactly opposite Luna Park, close to the Ramat Gan stadium. The Maimadion opens from June to September on Shabbat and holidays from 09.00 to 17.00.

Sderot Rokach

Tel. 03-642-2777

http://www.meymadion.co.il

5) Tel Aviv is always good for a surprise and most surprising is that the city has an ice-skating rink: **Iskate.**

Located inside Luna Park, you can find it at Gate 8.

It is open all year round, also during the week:

15.00-22.00 (Shabbat open at 10.00)

Sderot Rokach

Tel. 03-641-8418 http://www.iskate-lunapark.co.il

6) The **Zoo (Safari)** is situated in Ramat Gan and "Safari" is not the only its name, it is what it is. Apart from the zoo section, there are wild animals that can be observed either from within your own car or a safari bus. The park opens daily at 09.00 and lets visitors in until the early afternoon. Guided safaris are offered, like the "Morning Safari" that starts early in the morning and gives the participants the chance to observe the animals before the park opens. The tour can be booked with or without breakfast. A similar offer can be booked for the evening. Children must be at least 3 years old to participate in a safari. On Shabbat, the safari train crosses the park.

1 Sderot HaZvi, Ramat Gan

Tel. 03-630-5328/7/6

http://www.safari.co.il

8.3   Restaurants

I SRAEL IS VERY CHILD-FRIENDLY and it is not really necessary to search for a special restaurant to eat out with the youngest family members. But there are two places which go an extra mile for children: **MOSES** and the **DYADA** Center. Moses is a good bistro-restaurant which offers coloring books, play corner, kid's menu, etc. The Dyada Center organizes different kinds of family activities from first day of pregnancy until first day in school. The bistros focus on the needs of both children and parents. Unfortunately the website is only in Hebrew, except a general information page in English) but emails are answered promptly.

7) **Moses**: 35, Rothschild Blvd., Tel. 03-566.4949, http://www.mosesrest.co.il/

8) **Dyada**: 75, Ben Gurion Blvd.

9) Tel Aviv Port Hangar 17–18, einatg@dyada.co.il, http://www.dyada.co.il.

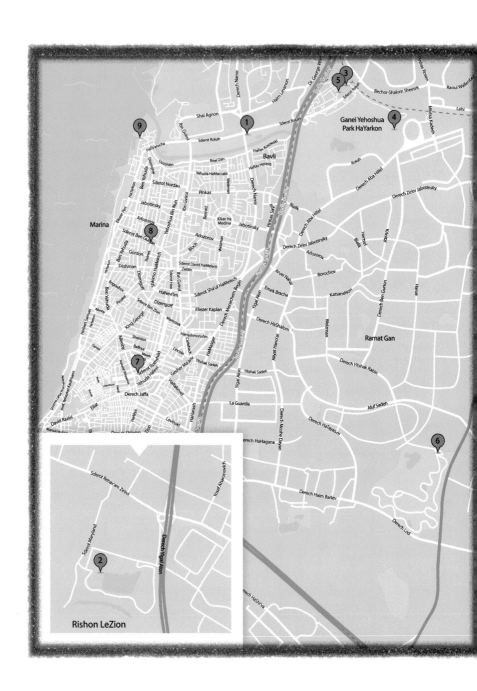

9

Eating Out

T EL AVIV'S RESTAURANTS ARE among the most creative and
exotic in the world. This special fusion of Jewish traditional
food influenced by the immigrants' home countries like Poland,
Russia, Morocco, Persia, etc., created a totally new cuisine of
"Ethno Food," spiced with the Near East flavor. It is nearly impossible to not eat well in Israel. Even the cocktail bars offer more
than just snacks. Every restaurant offers a lunch menu and in the
upper class restaurants, these are real bargains in comparison to
the prices in the evening. Tip is about 15 percent.

Israelis eat more than they drink and there is practically no
bar that does not cater some snacks. Most bars call themselves
resto-bars and what they offer is actually more than a simple
snack– even at a late hour. While restaurants tend to describe
the food on the menu, the street food is for the savvy. Here is
some gastro-vocabulary:

Sabiḥ is served in pita bread that is filled with mashed and fried
eggplants, sesame cream, a boiled egg, salad etc., as you like. Ever
since sabiḥ was introduced to the local food market by Iraqi Jews,
nobody wants to miss it.

Similar to sabiḥ, **falafel** is also served in pita bread but instead
of the eggplant, the falafel contains fried balls from chickpeas

and/or fava beans, sesame cream and pickles as well as tomatoes, onions, etc., add what you like.

Shavarma comes in different varieties depending on the type of meat and dressing. The thin meat layers are stuffed into the pita bread and the other ingredients are similar to sabi*h* and falafel, and if you want, you can even add some fries on top.

Hummus is made from mashed chickpeas and tahini, lemon juice and olive oil are added as well as garlic and salt. It is served with pita bread. Every Israeli has his/her favorite Hummus shop; in Tel Aviv, most are located in the south.

Shakshuka is a pan dish mixing fresh tomatoes, herbs, onions, sometimes also chili before eggs are finally added. Originally from Northern Africa, Shakshuka has become the Israeli national dish. Most hotels have it on their buffet.

Where to eat?
Of course, this depends. The longer you live in Tel Aviv, the more you will become an expert yourself. The following places attract a large audience with what they have to offer:

1) Dizengoff Center – Food Court
Thursdays from 12.00-21.00 and Fridays from 10.00-16.00 the Dizengoff Center turns into a food court with wonderful snacks and delicatessen. The Gan Meir Park is close by; this is the perfect opportunity for a picnic.

2) Sabiẖ and Falafel
You cannot miss it: right on the corner of Frishman and Dizengoff

Street you will see a long line of people waiting for their food.

Hummus

Everybody claims to know the best Hummus place. The traditional shops open in the morning and once the fresh Hummus is sold, they close again, normally in the early evening, or even before.

3) Abu Hassan

This is a classic. Abu Hassan has been around for ages and can be considered a landmark. The place opens at 8.00 in the morning and by 15.00 is already closed again, all the hummus is sold. You can dine in or take it home. 1 HaDolfin St. Ajami, border with Jaffa.

4) Abu Dubby

Hummus with Jamaica flavor. At Abu Dubby, you may enjoy your hummus together with reggae music, even on Shabbat. 81 King George St. 81/ Bar Giora.

Shakshuka

You will find it on nearly every menu and in your hotel buffet

even in the morning. But one restaurant you must not miss: Dr. Shakshuka.

5) Dr. Shakshuka

You can either go to the uncrowned shakshuka king from Tripoli (3 Beit Eshel St. near Clock Tower, Tel. 057-944-4193), or try a relatively new shakshuka place:

6) Rico Shakshuka Bar

It is a little children-friendly bistro in the upcoming district of Florentin (45 Abarbanel St). Tel. 050-229-4212

Is all that kosher?

Tel Aviv is a very secular city and not all restaurants are kosher (in Hebrew: ka-shér, meaning: suitable), but many are. If you are still wondering why there is no cheese on the salami pizza or why that cheese is artificial, here is a little introduction to the Jewish dietary laws, called *kashrut* (speak: kash-root)

What is kashrut?

Kashrut is dietary law. It prescribes which foods maybe eaten at all, especially which animals (see 3rd book of Moses). It is not allowed to consume blood, and meat and dairy have to be strictly separated from each other (no cheese burger, no cordon bleu allowed). Neutral foods are "parve," meaning not dairy, not meat, e.g., vegetables and fruits. Cheese is a difficult product since it is made with the help of lab-ferment, traditionally coming from animals, but nowadays it is possible to make hard cheese from microbial lab-ferment.

How do I know whether it is kosher?

Kosher food is labeled as are restaurants. The label can also be found on products that are naturally kosher like wine, but where the production in an un-kosher factory could add impurities. The label is supervised by the rabbinate. In the US, you often find on the products the letter "U" from the Orthodox Union. In other countries, it might look like a stamp and shows the name of the certifier.

9.1 Coffee & Cafés

I SRAELIS LOVE COFFEE AND dispute with Spaniards and Italians who makes the best. The big Israeli coffee shop chain AROMA CAFÉ (black logo, white and red letters) offers not only hot drinks and cakes but also salads and sandwiches. At the Port (Nemal) of Tel Aviv, you will find a couple of cafés next to the water where you can sit down on the big wooden step and enjoy a coffee or while contemplating the sea.

Do you drink your coffee with milk? You might want to try an "upside-down coffee," called coffee afuch, where the milk sits on top of the coffee. In summer, you will find many cafés offering "coffee barad," in Europe called frappé, with crushed ice. The Israelis have a product even for the lovers of Turkish coffee: the "mud coffee," coffee botz. Turkish coffee is put together with sugar into the cup and hot water added.

7) In **Bakery 29** (29, Ahad Ha'am) Netta Korin realized her dream. After many successful years in Wall Street, she came back to Tel

Aviv to open this bakery-café and support social projects. The venue is very stylish and modest at the same time.

Every day from 07.30 and 20.00 (Friday until sunset), the kitchen creates wonderful sweet and savory snacks.

Closed on Shabbat.

Tel. 03-560-2020.

http://www.bakery29.com

8) Dellal is not only an exquisite restaurant; they also have an excellent bakery-café close by (7, Kol Israel Haverim). Mousses, éclairs, tarts, quiches... the most exquisite pastries lie at your feet. A great place to have a coffee in the center of Neve Tzedek.

9) Founded in 1919 by Moshe Landwer from Berlin, Landwer was Israel's first coffee brand. The **Café Landwer** is an old classic in Tel Aviv. It has become a chain with several venues in the city. The nicest are in the Gan Meir Park (7 Rabenu Tam St). This little oasis seems to be far away from the buzzing city and invites you to stay for a coffee and some cake or sandwich, or soup, or....
Café Landwer
Tel. 03-629-5870.
Other addresses are:
98 Dizengoff (next to Frishman St).
70 Ibn Gvirol 70 (south of city hall)
45 Rothschild (Ramhal St).
14 Eliezer Peri St. (Marina, behind Gordon Pool)

10) **Max Brenner** (45, Rothschild Blvd. and in the port) is the name of Tel Aviv's chocolate planet. Chocolate in all varieties (to eat, to drink, hot, cold, spiced, black, white...) can be found on the menu and in the shop. Max Brenner also offers a creative selection of sandwiches, pasta, entrecotes and salads.
Tel. 03-560-4570.

11) **Café Mia** (55, Shabazi St) is a charming little café in Neve Tzedek that managed to preserve its flair despite of its popularity. Mia offers good coffee with tasty cakes as well as sandwiches and salads.
Tel. 03-576-8793.

12) Sitting in **Ninas Café** (29, Shabazi St). It feels like being at a friend's place. Owner Eliza Zibi imported the French café flair to Tel Aviv. The waiters wear white shirts and black vests; the style of the café is very classy but also intimate. The black-and-white

photos show the owner's friends and family. Eliza orchestrated the café herself and the results are handmade cakes and fresh little dishes.

Tel. 03-516-1767

http://ninacafehotel.com.

13) The port of Jaffa is the home of the **Café Kapish** which is part of the Na Laga'at Center (see Theaters). Open every day from 09.00 to 23.00, the café offers not only a great Israeli breakfast in a place a bit off the beaten path but also amazing cocktails (try the apple-jito or kir royal with pomegranate). The highlights of the menu are the cheese cake with strawberry sauce, the pasta and the hummus.

14) Even McDonald's is allowed to be part of this selection. The coffee of the Israeli **McCafé** (33,Rothschild Blvd). is good, the staff is friendly and the big terrace on the lower Rothschild Blvd. is a fantastic place to have a coffee in a prime location.

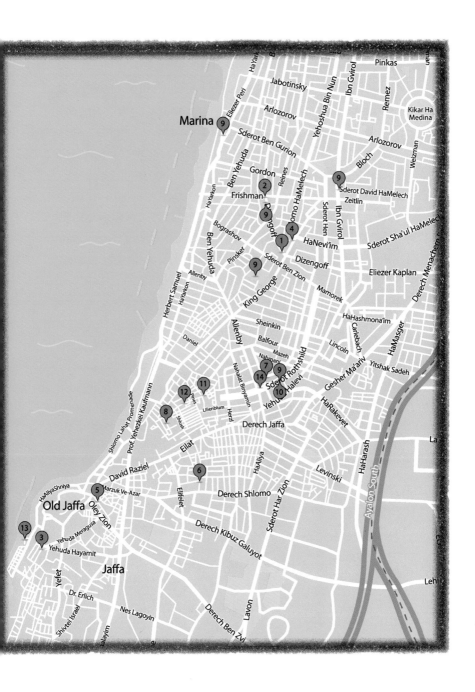

9.2 Restaurants

T HE ISRAELI DRESS CODE is rather casual, but always cool. This is important. Nobody will turn you away only because you are wearing jeans or the wrong label. Even outdoor sandals are not a general no-go, but: the better the restaurant, the less people are willing to see outdoor.

Even though you can pay with credit card in nearly all places, little neighborhood eateries will not likely accept them. Here are some recommendations to have the ultimate local gourmet experience:

Yemenite
The following selected Yemenite restaurants are little family eateries around the Carmel Market where the neighborhood has lunch at reasonable prices. In the little streets around the market, you will discover even more. The tasty food is served with bread and spicy sauces (*skhug*). Having lunch here will make you feel like a local. Between 12.00 and 13.30, the places are very full and you might have to wait a bit for a table.

1) Eres
24 Nahliel St.
Tel. 03-510-2555
Great quality for little money. Probably one of the best shnitzels in town.

2) Rina & Zacharia
22 HaKovshim St.
Their soups are legendary and the house specializes in typical

Yemenite food with a variety of meat.

Eastern

3) Odelia
89 Ben Yehuda St. or 1, Daniel Frisch St

4) HaPina Shel Chaim ("Chaim's corner")
33 Basel St. also belongs to the group of neighborhood restaurants.
As if granny was cooking for you...

5) Jamilla
31 Gruzenberg St. spoils her guests with delicacies from the
Moroccan cuisine like couscous and different chicken dishes.
Unfortunately, the place closes already at 18.00.

6) In Shamaya
2 Vital St. the owner is the chef himself. His eastern dishes are
of considerable size and are served with a generous side dish.
Closed on Shabbat.
Tel. 03-682-9217.

Fusion/ Mediterranean
The Jewish immigration from different countries has left its mark
on the local cuisine and over the years, the chefs have created
dishes nobody wants to miss.

7) Gedera 26
26 Gedera St. is so very much "Big Orange": all nationalities seem
to have passed through the kitchen. Gedera 26 is an upscale
restaurant; a main course costs about 60-90 NIS. Closed from

Friday afternoon until Monday.
Tel. 03-510-0164.

8) Cheder Ha Ochel (means "dining room")

23 Shaul Ha Melech Blvd. and is located at the Tel Aviv Performing Art Center (TAPAC). Have a seat at the long tables and enjoy the company. The restaurant presents itself in a very modest style and focuses on the food which comes like tapas in little portions. Due its proximity to the opera, this place is very full shortly before and after the performance.
Tel. 03-696-6188.

9) Puah

3 Rabbi Yochanan St. Close to the flea market, next to the antiquities merchants. The friendly bistro-restaurant is decorated with many unique items and they are all for sale. Puah has a heart for vegetarians, but the menu offers something for everybody's taste. Price 75 NIS per person.
Tel. 03-682-3821.

10) Coffee Bar

13 Haruzim St. The name is a discreet understatement for a restaurant in the budgetary upper middle class. Located since 1994 in an area where not many go for a stroll, the Coffee Bar has become one of the best restaurants in town.
It is open 7 days a week; breakfast is served from 09.00-12.00, except on Shabbat when a special family lunch is offered.
From Sun.-Thurs. they offer a business lunch from 12.00-17.00, the dinner follows on seamlessly.
Tel. 03-688-9696.

Lunch in the Yemenite Quarter

Outside

11) Susanna

8 Shabazi St. The neighborhood without it is impossible! In the heart of Neve Tzedek, a beautiful terrace offers a shady refuge on those hot days. Whether you are simply looking for a nice cup of good coffee or a large dinner, Susanna's kitchen is delicious and also suitable for vegetarians! In summer they open the roof terrace. With a drink in your hand, you can now enjoy the village flair of this beautiful old neighborhood.
Tel. 03-517-7580.

12) The Bellini

6 Yechieli St. is located close to the Suzanne Dellal Center. A nice Italian family restaurant on a quiet side street with a shady terrace. Open every day from 12.00 to midnight, the Bellini offers a very good menu with renowned Italian food and dishes from "la mamma." Every day, there is a different lunch special or you can eat à la carte. The main dishes start around 65 NIS.
Tel. 057-943-9619.

13) Martha's Kitchen and Wine bar

26 Ibn Gvirol St. The elegant leather sofas give the restaurant the flair of an English club, but the kitchen is truly Mediterranean and the wine list extensive. The place is famous for its vodkas, e.g., with lavender-lemon flavor. The restaurant has a nice garden which is situated away from the street and turns the venue into a little oasis on Tel Aviv's Broadway. The main dishes start at ca. 70 NIS.
Tel. 057-944-1143.

14) Vicky Cristina is a tapas bar and restaurant in the old train station HaTachana. The wine bar curls around the big old tree and the guests enjoy Spanish rhythm, beautiful decor, food (from Vicky) and wine (from Cristina) as if they were in Spain. Wine is their specialty; the list contains 120 different names.
Tel. 03-736-7272.

Jewish/ Eastern-European

15) The **Eli Melech**
35 Wolfson St. It feels really homey and worth the trip to the end of Herzl St. in Florentin. If you want to practice Yiddish, this is your place: there is no menu other than in Yiddish and Hebrew. Actually you do not have to read the menu anyway, just order their gefilte fish or cholent and you will want to come back next day.
Tel: 03-681-4545

16) Little Prague

56 Allenby St. is more a pub than a restaurant but also offers typical Czech food like goulash, shnitzel, walnut cake with lemon icing, etc., and, of course, many Czech beers.
Tel. 03- 516-8137.

17) Kiton

145 Dizengoff St. opened in the 1940s and legend has it that the menu is still the same: kugel (sweet noodle gratins), fish, soups..., well-proven typical East-European, Jewish cuisine.
Tel. 03-523-3679.

18) Nanuchka

30 Lilienblum St. is a legendary Georgian restaurant with a special flair: nice furniture, fresh flowers and old porcelain with flower design. The guests quickly feel at home and at the end of the evening, most have made new friends or dance on the bar. The later the hour, the better the party. The kitchen is very creative: when local ingredients meet Georgian tradition, the result is amazing like the spring roll "Black Sea." Main dishes start at about 55 NIS and the lunch menu at 49 NIS.
Tel. **03-516.2254**

Vegetarian/Vegan

19) Café Birnbaum

31 Nachalat Binyamin St. belongs to a small group of restaurants that are at least as old as the State of Israel, if not older. Every day (except for Shabbat,) the Birnbaum prepares a great salad buffet and home-made cakes. The café opens in the morning and closes (unfortunately) in the late afternoon.

20) Buddha Burgers

21 Yehuda Ha Levi St. or 86 Ibn Gvirol St. makes health junkies happy: for every dish, you can consult the nutrition facts and ingredients. The menu is very international: burritos, tortilla rolls, sushi, salad, soups, pasta, cakes, etc. Main courses start at 25 NIS. BB is closed on Shabbat, but open till midnight the rest of the week.

Gluten-free

21) Mezze

51 Achad Ha'am St. is God-sent for all those who (have to) eat gluten-free. Even though it is a general vegetarian restaurant, it offers at least one main dish (start at 40 NIS) and several desserts that are gluten-free.

Open daily from 08.00-24.00, Fridays only until 17.30, closed on Shabbat.

Tel. 03-629-9753.

Meat

Most Tel Aviv restaurants offer a very good meat quality, but some of them should not be missed by carnivores:

22) Nomen est omen, **Makom Shel Basar** means "Place of Meat"

64 Shabazi St. and here they demand a great deal of their own meat production. The restaurant has its own rooms and equipment for meat hanging and additional processing. The excellent wine selection makes the menu perfect. Makom Shel Basar is located close to Rothschild Blvd. where Neve Tzedek starts. Guests can also enjoy their meal on a very nice terrace.

Meat dishes start at 130 NIS. Tel. 03-510.4021.

23) Rak Basar – "Only Meat"

19 Derech Salameh/Shelma is the motto of this meat restaurant and this is the understatement of the century! Eating at Rak Basar is a great experience. Like in a butcher's shop, the guest can choose the piece with the help from an expert. Like in Makom Shel Basar, the meat is produced in-house and sold by weight. Tel. 03-681-3590.

24) Yo'ezer Wine Bar

2 Yo'ezer Ish Habira St. (close to clock tower) is renowned for its meat quality. No wonder you have to reserve a table beforehand. Candles and wooden furniture turn this charming wine cellar in Jaffa into a very cozy place.

The lunch menu is flexible and depending on the type of meat, it costs between 88 and 166 NIS; alternatively the guest can order a noodle dish for 74 NIS.

On the regular menu, an excellent entrecote is offered for 199 NIS. Tel. 03-683-9115.

More good addresses for meat are Moses, Moses Station and Agadir Burger.

25) Moses: 35 Rothschild Blvd. (Restaurant).

26) Moses Station: 293 Dizengoff St. (Burger-Bar).

27) Agadir Burger: 2 Nachalat Binyamin (Burger-Bar).

Beach

28) Manta Ray is the restaurant with the "killer location" as critics call it: Alma Beach between Charles Clore Park and Etzel Museum. The prices are still very reasonable for such an excellent eastern restaurant (main dishes start at 85 NIS). The Manta Ray

considers itself a fish restaurant but they also serve good entrecote and even vegetarian dishes. Every day from 09.00 to 12.00, you can enjoy a wonderful breakfast with pancakes, omelet, fruit, champagne... and beach! In the afternoons, you can enjoy the beach and later, the sunset with coffee and an amazing dessert (e.g., caramelized figs) and a good drink.
Tel. 03-517-4773.

29) Herbert Samuel

6 Koifman St. was rated best Tel Aviv restaurant in 2010. It is not located right on the beach, but the sea view is fantastic. The cuisine is Mediterranean, very creative and the dishes are served in a very beautiful presentation. For lunch, the Herbert Samuel offers a 3-course-menu for 110 NIS. Every Sunday evening, the restaurant goes east: "Hot Indian Sunday."
Tel. 03-5166516.

Exquisite

30) Mul Yam means "across the sea"

Hangar 24 Tel Aviv Port. It is the best fish restaurant in the whole of Israel and, therefore, the only Israeli restaurant that is listed in the gourmet guide "Les Tables du Monde," and deservedly so. Do not forget to order a Fabergé Egg! Business lunch is served every day – even Sundays and holidays – for 160 NIS and175 NIS respectively. In the evening, they open at 19.30, the main courses start at about 200 NIS.
Tel. 03-546-9920.

31) Catit

4 Hayal HaTalmud St. is one of the most exclusive places in town.

Chef Meir Adon turns even the simplest of dishes into a gourmet meal, whether it is a Spanish almond gazpacho or sushi. Business lunch is offered for 139 NIS. Tel. 03-510-7001.

32) Messa

19 HaArba'a St. is the stylish restaurant of Chef Aviv Moshe. His specialty is the Nouvelle French Cuisine with creations like a caramelized fish with tempura avocado and lychee jelly. Main dishes start at 100 NIS. You need to reserve your table 2 days in advance! Open daily from 12.00-15.30 and 19.00-24.00. Tel. 03-685-6859.

33) Dallal

10 Shabazi St. travels back with you into the time when Neve Tzedek was a place for Jewish entrepreneurs who had decided to leave the then-claustrophobic and crowded Jaffa to build their new homes here. This romantic restaurant was built on the ruins of three old houses, with an intimate courtyard and open air bar. The menu is well balanced between fish and meat dishes and an additional dish of the day. The prices are still reasonable: breakfast 55 NIS, main courses start at 80 NIS and the "Executive Lunch" is offered for 70-110 NIS. Tel. 057-943-9499.

Breakfast

Israelis appreciate a good breakfast and nearly all restaurants start the day latest at 09.00 with a breakfast menu, whether it is the **Manta Ray** or the **Café Landwer**, they are all prepared for hungry early morning guests. The restaurant **Dallal** has even its own bakery and café, but the most renowned place for breakfast is **Benedict.**

34) Benedict – "All about breakfast"
29 Rothschild Blvd. or 171 Ben Yehuda St. Their slogan says it all. Benedict serves breakfast 24/7: pancakes, champagne, orange juice, croissants, eggs ... the perfect start to the day!
Tel. 03-686-8657.

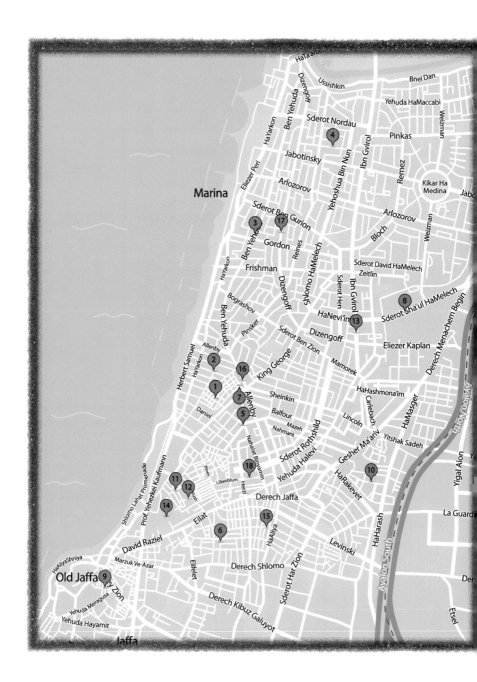

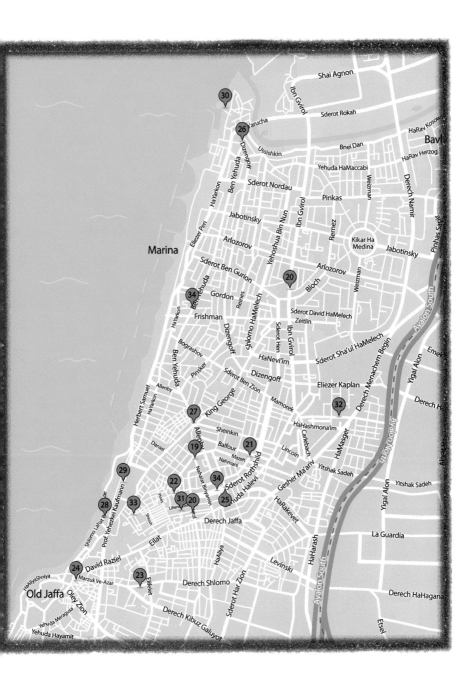

10
Nightlife

TEL AVIV CALLS ITSELF "the city that never stops" and this is not the whole story. Tel Aviv never stops and keeps changing within seconds; a permanent balancing act between Near Eastern lifestyle and European roots. "Being cool" is the most important task; "tradition" nearly an offense. Bars, clubs and restaurants come and go; the city shows a new face in every moment. Just one thing never changes: the late hour. Before 23.00, nothing is really going on and this is still early.

Wednesday is the best day to make sure you meet more locals than tourists. Sunday is the first work day of the week and everything is just one day earlier. Meaning: Thursday and Fridays are really full and Saturday, Shabbat, is quieter because everybody has to go back to work the next day.

Beverages
If you want to get a taste of the local lifestyle, why not order an arrak-grapefruit long drink? Tel Aviv summers are hot and a cool beer, whether Maccabi or Goldstar, is always welcome. In recent years, the wines from the Golan Heights have gained presence and have also been internationally awarded.

Smoking
Smoking in public is quite restricted also in Israel nowadays. Since 2007, bars and restaurants have to offer non-smoking areas or

they will be fined. But Tel Aviv is very generous and controls are much more relaxed than in the rest of the country; a national commission rebuked the municipality in September 2011 for its lax attitude. Rule of thumb: before you light your cigarette, have a look around what the others are doing; if controls are being imposed, both the bar owner and the smoking customer pay a fine.

10.1 Bars

T EL AVIV'S NIGHTLIFE IS abundant and it is very difficult to make a decision about where to go. Sometimes, it feels like there is a new bar opening every day. If you are new in town, you can start with bar hopping around Lilienblum Street and from there explore Florentin. In the hot summers, the Tel Aviv port invites you to have a cool beer or sophisticated drink in one of the many open air bars. Dizengoff and Ibn Gvirol are also good for a decent pub crawl. You don't have to be an insider to enjoy a night out in Tel Aviv.

Beachfront

1) Shalvata is a great location to start the evening or to stay all night. Centrally located in the Tel Aviv port, this place is often very crowded. Come early for an aperitif, have dinner, then go to the bar to enjoy a good drink, all while having a sea view and good music.
Tel. 057-944.2873.

2) The **Carlton Hotel**
10 Eliezer Peri St., Hilton Beach offers a superb refuge for hot summer evenings: from their beach bar, the guests will have a nice view of the marina; the ambiance is classy and stylish paired with perfect service and ambitious cocktails.

3) LaLa Land
131 Herbert Samuel St., Gordon Beach is a typical beach bar and cannot be missed. At any time of day, LaLa Land provides the ultimate holiday feeling: feet in the sand, drinks, sea view. The kitchen serves good hummus, typical Israeli snacks and a memorable chocolate cake.

North

4) 223
223 Dizengoff St. / Basel St. is one of the coolest bars of its kind. The cocktail design is so smart that you might hesitate to drink them. The bar was founded by six local bar tenders and the result

is very worthwhile seeing. Every Saturday night, the bar invites the guests to participate in the "Tiki Night." Aloha!

Tel. 03-544-6537

https://www.facebook.com/223bar

5) Meir Bar

190 Dizengoff St. is easy to miss. It is located in a little street off Dizengoff. The bar has a very personal touch and is definitely not mainstream which also shows on the surprisingly large beer and wine list and the tapas they serve. Different DJs take care of the entertainment for the 30+ audience; Tuesday is for the Jewish Genre lovers. Ever dreamed of being a bar man? Come on Wednesdays and give it a try.

Mon.-Sat. 21.00-04.00.

Tel. 052-885-6619

Center

6) La Champa

16 HaArba'a St. is a Catalan Cava bar (if you can ignore that they speak Castellano and not Català) with a great Cava, nice tapas and a flag of good old Catalunya with a donkey on it. The staff is very friendly and helps you with recommendations through the Hebrew tapas menu.

Tel. 077-200-8636.

7) Abraxas

40 Lilienblum St. is one of the most popular bars on the party mile of Lilienblum Street. Much has been written and said about Abraxas; fact is: it is still there. The snacks are good, the bar too, the guests are even more beautiful and the DJs make you dance.

No particular dress code.
Tel. 03-510-4435.

8) Lima Lima

42 Lilienblum St. is much bigger than it looks from outside. It is a mainstream bar and discotheque that reflects the flavor of the moment. The place is open every day; Monday is "Gay Night." Tel. 03-560.0924.

9) Evita

31 Yavne St. claims to be the city's oldest gay bar. Everybody is welcome whether straight, gay, lesbian, bi or transsexual. Their "Eurovision Sundays" are just about the limit!
Tel. 03-566-9559.

10) Gilda

62 Ahad Ha'am St. is a cozy little bar close to Rothschild Boulevard and some people's extended living room. Here, you will meet locals who were just looking for a relaxed place where the music invites them to chill and the bartenders make the right decisions. Of course, the food is delicious, too.
Tel. 03-560-3588.

11) The entrance of the Otto 76

76 Ibn Gvirol seems to be extra hard to find: pass the roller shutter and the green cage. Once in, a very modern and stylish club opens its doors to you. The DJs play popular music (80s, 90s, current hits), the bar is good and the audience is roughly between 20 and 40. Dress code: between relaxed and stylish.
Tel. 077-414-5043.
You will find other "Ottos" here:

46 Ahad Ha'am

302 Dizengoff St.

South

12) The little Satchmo
6 Vital St. has its priorities right: good music and good whiskey.
Opens daily at 20.00.
Tel. 052-328-4800.

13) Jajo
40 Shabazi St. is an intimate bar in the heart of Neve Tzedek.
Surrounded by modest background music, the guests easily fall
in love with the excellent wine list. Daily from 19.00, Fridays
from 13.00-20.00.
Tel. 03-516-4557

14) Bugsy
26 Florentine St. has already been here now for several years,
which is quite an achievement in Tel Aviv. The guests love the
combination of modernity, good food, moderate prices and
sophisticated drinks (they have 14 different vodkas!) Maybe try
it first for breakfast: wonderful pancakes with maple syrup! Opens
daily at 09.00, Shabbat at 10.00.
Tel. 057-944-0882.

15) Perla
8 Florentin St. is a friendly bar for a younger crowd: dimly lit,
mainstream music, much alcohol, and high spirits.
Tel. 03-68-3823.

Jaffa

16) Container

Warehouse 2 is located in the Jaffa port right next to the fishermen's boats. It is a restaurant, bar and art space in one with different DJs. Tables with white tablecloth and blue wooden chairs fit perfectly in the old port. The bar is made out of a real container, currently the "place to be."
Tel. 03-683-6321.

17) Jaffa Bar

30 Yefet St. belongs to Chef Nir Tzuk (Cordelia restaurant, across from the bar) and spoils guests with excellent snacks and noble alcohol. The bar is located on a side street in an Ottoman building. The warm, original style transports you to bygone eras in Old Jaffa. Opens daily at 20.00.
Tel. 03-518-4668.

18) Shafa Bar

2 Rabbi Nachman MiBreslev St. is located in the south of Jaffa. It is a very relaxed place; most of the guests like an alternative lifestyle and the bar offer good music and little snacks. Sometimes, the music comes from the guests themselves, the piano is just waiting for you to play it.

19) Saloona Art Bar

17 Tirzeh St. is an appreciated relief from the usual bar scene. Not only do they exhibit art, they also invite different singers and bands. Every day from 21.00 on, you can enjoy a creative art bar with even more creative snacks.
Tel. 03-518-1719.

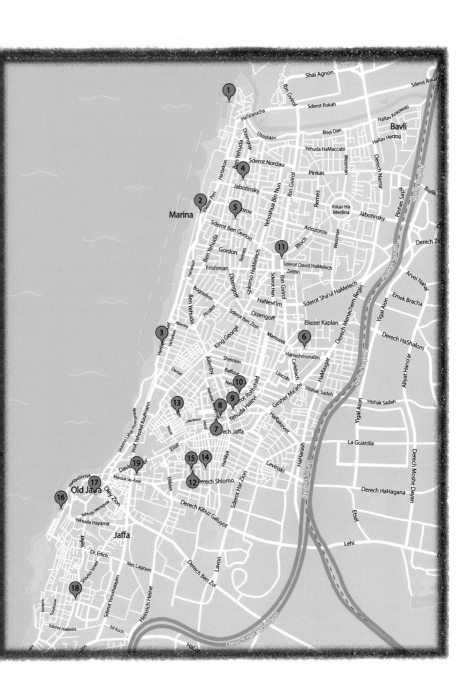

10.2 Clubs

I T IS DIFFICULT TO say where exactly the bar turns into a club. In Tel Aviv, they distinguish between bars and "mega bars": a bar with a dance floor. You can find many of them on YouTube, so you have an idea before you go.

North

1) Galina is a very popular club with beautiful people.
Located in Hangar 19 in the port of Tel Aviv, the club gets really crowded and people dance around the bar. If this is too much for you, just step out for a moment and enjoy the sea view.
Tel. 03-544-5553.

2) Zappa Club
24 Raoul Wallenberg St. is a bit off the beaten path, in the north of the city. Good music, entertaining live performances and – like everywhere – nice snacks, of course. The club opens at 20.30, but nothing is really moving before 22.00.
Tel. 03-762-6666.

Center North

3) Zizi Club
7, Carlebach St. loves Electro. On Thursdays, the music is mixed and satisfies the mainstream audience. On Fridays, it's time for PAG, the gay parties.
Tel. 03-561-1597.

4) House and techno lovers will like the underground club
Penguin
43 Yehuda Halevi St. The club starts "late"; translation: afterhours.
Open from Monday to Friday. Do not hesitate to go into the
shabby entrance; as mentioned above, it is an underground club.
Tel. 054-485-2741.

5) YaYa Club
1 Ben Yehuda St. is a quite new venue in Tel Aviv. It opened in 2011
and was instantly a huge success. Located in a high-rise building
called Migdalor, the YaYa Club offers good music to the mainstream clubber. Not to mention the roof terrace... Club motto:
"We make fun funner." Opens daily at 21.00, Shabbat at 18.00.
Tel. 050-444-6664.

South

6) The star of the Block Club
157 Derech Shalma <Salameh> is always the performing musician, not the bar. Many of the world's greatest DJs had their Israel debut in this club, like Henrik Schwarz in October 2011.

7) Ha'oman 17
88, Abarbanel St. belongs to the best in all of Israel and is also one of the biggest. On Thursdays and Fridays, this club is the meeting place for the international DJ world (e.g., Paul van Dyk, Paul Oakenfold, etc). The club is a landmark in Tel Aviv nightlife. Tel. 03-681-3636.

11
Shopping

TEL AVIV LIVES A double life between the Near East and Europe and shopping is a special experience. The absence of a true eastern bazaar in Tel Aviv does not stop the locals from behaving as if. Everything is negotiable. It does not hurt to ask, e.g., if there is a discount if you pay cash or take more than one item. The more politely you ask, the better your chances. The following streets are worth strolling down to get an impression of the local offers. Every shop, but definitely every shopping center has its own security personnel. The little boutiques might not have anybody at their door, but most places are blocked by a security gate where your belongings are screened and bags opened. Israelis know the procedure and normally there are no lines.

Allenby Street

During the 1920s, this was the most commercial street in Tel Aviv. Erwin Moses, son of the Jewish doctor and Member of Parliament Dr. Julius Moses, opened here in the 1930s the shop "The Gentleman," a haberdasher. Erwin Moses had immigrated to Palestine already in the early 1930s, but little is left from this period. Many houses seem to be only weeks away from collapsing but still stand like proud witnesses of golden times gone by. Vintage and second-hand shops, book merchants and shoe shops and somehow a little bit of everything can be found here.

Bograshov Street
Unlike Allenby Street, on Bograshov, the focus is more on clothes, including second-hand and vintage.

Dizengoff Street
For Jews from Berlin and Budapest, Dizengoff Street was a worthy substitute for the Kurfürstendamm. They had left their countries involuntarily and felt alien in the Near East, but not on Dizengoff. On Shabbat, they would come here for a walk, have a coffee in one of the many cafés and mingle with other Europeans. The Hebrew language even developed its own verb for this: *le-hiz-dangef*, to hang out in Dizengoff. The upper part (above Frishman St.) has always attracted customers with high spending power but in recent years, competition has shown up: Kikar HaMedina.

Kikar HaMedina
It is the ultimate luxury address and as mentioned before, the competition of Northern Dizengoff. Many residents of the nearby Ramat Aviv (Northern District of Tel Aviv) work in Israel's booming high-tech industry. These shops are not short of clients.

Gan HaHashmal
Around the electricity garden (in Hebrew: Gan HaHashmal), former home of the first power plant, an interesting transformation has been taking place. The once neglected neighborhood is blossoming again and is now a must for fashion lovers: many little shops and showrooms from innovative young designers can be found here. Gan HaHashmal is surrounded by the streets of Yehuda HaLevy, HaRakevet, Menachem Begin and Allenby.

Sheinkin Street

Sheinkin is legendary. Israel's leftwing scene lives here. The 1968 generation has gotten grey hair, but Sheinkin is still a relaxed place with alternative lifestyles, political discussions and an interesting mix of shops with Indian imports, incense sticks, organic food and informal clothes.

Shabazi Street

Neve Tzedek is full of little treasures and some are hidden here in these little streets: fashion, jewelry and crafts and always a nice bistro or café in between.

Tchernichovsky Street

This street is totally underestimated and hardly mentioned as a shopping destination. Tchernichovsky seems to be quiet and not commercial at all. Those who are ready for a surprise will discover little boutiques, and not only for women. At the corner of Allenby Street, you will find some nice bistros.

Jaffa

Old Jaffa specializes in tourism while the streets around the flea market attract young designers who give the ancient place a new coat of paint. Next to the flea market, there are more second-hand-shops: antiques, silver, carpets, etc. Bargaining is a must; you are in the Near East. Inside the shops, it is much quieter but nowhere else in the city are Europe and Orient so close.

11.1 Vintage/Second Hand

1) Mugraby is very typical for Allenby Street. It feels like digging into grandmother's closet and finding little treasures. The little Mugraby stretches over two floors; on the ground floor you can enjoy a relaxed cup of coffee. It opens early at 08.30.
32 Allenby St.
Tel. 03-525-4242.

2) Galérie Parisienne is a second-hand-designer-shop. Do not miss the basement where smaller wallets can also find something.
86 Frishman St.
Tel. 03-524-0793
E-mail: galerieparisienne.telaviv@gmail.com
http://www.galerieparisienne.com.

3) If you are looking for something really special and rare, **Retro-TLV** is your place for furniture, lamps and accessories. This shop is worth the visit!

123 Yehuda Halevi St.

Tel. 03-685-0663

http://www.retro-tlv.com.

4) In the "underground," which is the translation of **HaMartef** you can easily find well priced second-hand items.

2, King George St.

Tel. 03-528-3659

11.2 Fashion

5) The Israeli label **Frau Blau** was founded in 2002 by Helena Blaunstein and Philip Blau and soon became a major player in the Israeli fashion world. The design is fresh and modern, the special visual effects through print-ons are their trademark.

8 HaHashmal St.

Tel. 03-560-1735

http://www.fraublau.com.

6) Tanti Becky is another star of the local fashion scene. Vintage, their own creations, imported clothes, jewelry and furniture... visiting Tanti Becky is fun!

63 Bar Kochba St.

Tel. 03-525.5995

http://tantibecky.wordpress.com

https://www.facebook.com/tantibecky.

7) If you do not yet have any favorite pair of shoes, now you have no excuse anymore. At **Liebling Shoes**, you will find elegant leather shoes in a timeless design and high quality; limited edition.

63 Bar Kochba St.

Tel. 03-525-1020

http://www.liebling-shoes.com.

8) All shoes from **Achat-Achat** (UnaUna) are handmade and still reasonably priced. The minimal design and the quality of the fabrics turn each pair into a little work of art.

8 Rabbi Yochanan St.

Tel. 03-518-4782

http://una-una.com.

9) On Thursdays and Fridays, local designers show their creations on the **Dizengoff Center Designer Market** which is located on the ground floor. The market gives a nice overview of the local fashion scene without having to visit them all in their shops. Thurs. 16.00–21.00, Fri. 10.00–16.00.

11.3 Delicatessen

10) At **Bin281**, clerks spend much time with the client to make sure he buys a wine he will like. The atmosphere is relaxed and makes you want to further explore the world of grapes. In the wine bar on the second floor, you can enjoy not only a very good glass of wine but also a little snack while listening to relaxing music. 281 Dizengoff St., Tel. 03-544-4281

http://www.facebook.com\BIN.281
http://bin281.com.

11) The Food Market in the **Dizengoff Center** opens every Thursday afternoon and Friday morning. Here, you will find food from different origins. This is the time to get some lunch and have a picnic in the nearby Gan Meir Park. Dizengoff Square.

12) **Ahoti** (Hebrew for "My Sisters") operates the first fair trade shop in Israel. Ahoti is a charity which takes care of the wellbeing of women from non-European backgrounds. They organize education and professional training to ensure their economic independence. Ahoti acknowledges the women's ethnic background and offers them suitable programs. The founder is from Ethiopia which is reflected in many of the crafts in the shop. The shop sells nice bags, pottery, toys and also some delicatessen items like jam, herbs or oils. 4, Shlomo Hamelech St. Tel. 077-401-1271.

13) Nobody knows since when olive trees have been in Israel, but at **Olia** they know everything about olives and for this, they got an award at the International Food Fair SIAL in 2010. The shop is fascinating: olive oil products everywhere. In case your suitcase is full already, you can also shop online from home (nice website with recipes in English!) 73, Frishman St.
Tel. 03-522-3235
http://www.olia.co.il

11.4 Books

14) Steimatzky and books are synonymous in Israel. The Israeli chain is omnipresent and offers books in several languages, newspapers and travel maps. Some of the many shops are listed below:
· Dizengoff Center, Tel. 03-528-5271
· Allenby St. 107, Tel. 03-566-4277
· Sheinkin St. 45, Tel. 03-620-1495
E-mail: service@steimatzky.co.il
http://www.steimatzky.co.il (in Hebrew)

15) Halper's Books is a real highlight in the local second-hand book market. Located on busy Allenby Street, Halper's is well-known in the city by average people and notorious politicians. Halper's has received donations of whole book collections from "good families." Sun.-Thurs. 09.00-19.30, Fri. 09.00-16.00.

87 Allenby St.

Tel. 03-629-9710

E-mail:halpbook@netvision.co.il

http://www.halpersbooks.com

11.5 Music

16) "The Third Ear" – **HaOzen HaShlishit** – is a legend. The selection of new and used musical media is immense and the shop assistants are real experts. The Ozen Bar is part of the shop and live music is played in the evenings. The shop also serves as a box office. 48, King George St., Tel. 03-621.5223, info@third-ear. com, http://www.third-ear.com (in Hebrew).

17) At **Krembo Records**, a good music selection can readily be found. The shop belongs to a DJ and this is where you can also buy tickets for local dance parties.

96, Ben Yehuda St.,

Tel. 03-525.9507.

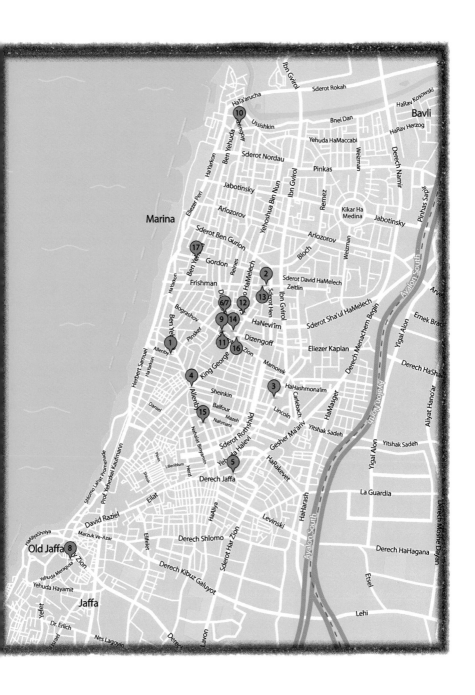

11.6 Miscellaneous

1) The old **HaTachana** train station where once the Jaffa-Jerusalem line stopped was refurbished some years ago and has become a nice place for having a coffee, strolling through little boutiques, enjoying some good tapas and a glass of wine. The official tourist information can also be found on the compound where they also have a little souvenir shop. The Tachana is located at the southern end of Kaufman St., right next to the IDF Museum. Kaufman St. /Mered St.
http://www.hatachana.co.il

Wellness
In such a vibrant and dynamic city like Tel Aviv, it is nearly impossible to just imagine a silent spot. When the feet are sore from all the walking or you simply need a breather, what about a relaxing massage or a pedicure?

2) In **Nature Spa** (Hebrew: *Teva spa*), little fish will kiss your feet in lukewarm water and leave the skin soft like baby's feet. The relaxing massage beds will recharge your battery. 100-102 Ben Yehuda St.
Tel. 03-522-3390
http://www.teva-spa.com
http://www.youtube.com/user/ourli.

3) The **DUO Spa** offers a professional Ayurvedic treatment, reflexology and shiatsu in a luxurious surrounding. After the treatment, you can stay at DUO and enjoy your new wellbeing.

As indicated in the name, DUO also offers the treatments for couples. The spa is open 7 days a week, at the weekend even until 01.00 in the morning.

106, Ha'Yarkon St.

Tel. 03-529-5333

E-mail: duo@duospa.co.il

http://www.duospa.co.il.

Diamonds

The best way to find a serious diamond dealer is to go the Diamond Exchange in Ramat Gan, right inside the eastern city limit: 1, Jabotinsky St., the Harry Oppenheimer Diamond Museum is also located here.

Judaica

Ben Yehuda St. is a good place to find a store for judaica. But there is one other shop that is worth being mentioned here:

4) **Minzer** is a Judaica shop that is targeting frumm Jews rather than tourists. Once inside, you might feel reminded of those little Jewish Judaica merchants in New York where you can buy religious books, sidurim, a new talit, etc. In this secular city, a shop like Minzer is quite an exception.

112 Allenby St. Tel. 03-560-5635

E-mail: binyamin81@neto.net.il

http://masoret.dpages.co.il (in Hebrew).

Souvenirs

What is typically Israeli? Only you can say which impressions you want take home. If there is no more space in your suitcase for olive oil and salt from the Dead Sea, what about magnets with pictures from Tel Aviv (e.g., in HaTachana) or a t-shirt? Israelis love printed t-shirts and the supply of t-shirts in English and Hebrew is abundant. You can also embroider something with your name in Hebrew, but his requires at least two days of advanced planning.

5) Monograma is well hidden in the little shopping center "London Mini-Store" on Ibn Gvirol. They embroider textiles with Hebrew letters and print photos on different things like cups, t-shirts and even flip-flops.

30 Ibn Gvirol St.

Tel. 03-696-2950

E-mail: monograma1@gmail.com

Hebrew website: http://www.monograma.co.il

6) Crazy Richard is the place to go to shop for Israeli army items.

Dizengoff Center (next to Gate 5)

Tel. 03-525-7465

http://www.israelmilitary.com

11.7 Markets

The markets in Tel Aviv are a treasure trove for rarities from different cultures and religions. A multitude of odors and flavors as diverse as the Israeli society fuse with nostalgia. Jews have lived all over the world for centuries and here in the markets, you can find something from every corner of the world.

Flea markets

7) Dizengoff Square Tues. 14.00–22.00, Fri. 09.00–16.00.

8) Shuk HaPishpeshim (English: flea market) in Jaffa is the oldest and surely the most outstanding market of the city. Here in Jaffa where Judaism, Islam and Christianity meet, life is colorful and vibrant. Whether in the halls or outside, in this market you'll find kitsch, design, antiques, good junk– just everything. Do not forget to bargain! If not in Jaffa, where? Friday is the most crowded day of the week and some say also the most expensive. On the side streets, there is more to see and buy from local merchants and nobody has ever starved here. For quite a while now, this area has been considered "trendy"; young designers, restaurants, bars... and new neighbors are not changing the face of Old Jaffa. This is now the best time to come for a visit. Nobody

knows how it will look years from now and whether this unique flair will survive.

Yefet St. /Oley Zion St., close to Clock Tower, Sun.–Thu. 10.00–18.00, Fri. 10.00–14.00.

9) On the northern side of lower King George St. close to Allenby St., you find the **Betzalel Market**, an open-air market with very cheap clothes from different origins. Open from Sunday to Friday until later afternoons; Fridays – like always – reduced opening hours.

Farmers' Markets

10) The **Carmel Market** is located next to the Yemenite Quarter, a market with an outstanding and colorful selection of fresh vegetables and fruits. In the afternoon, the food gets cheaper before they close down. In between, you find little bistros with falafel, shavarma, fresh fish, spices, dried fruit and hot tea. From here, you can continue to the Yemenite Quarter where you are certain to find a nice little place for lunch.

11) The everyday market is located inside the halls of the port of Tel Aviv, but every Friday, there is an additional farmers' market outside from 08.00-14.00. Sea view included! The prices are not as cheap as those at Carmel Market, but it has its very own flair and some products are even organic. The market is well worth a visit. Afterwards, you can have a coffee or second breakfast next to the sea.

12) The neighborhood around Levinsky St. is a bit rundown but full of life. When Jews were expelled from Arab countries in 1948 and came to Israel, many of them settled down in the south of the city. In the derelict houses between HaAliyah and Herzl St. (many of them from the 1930s,) today you will find merchants for spices, dried fruits, olives and also for delicatessen items. Lunch time is the best time for a visit. You can nearly always taste the food before you buy. Friday is the busiest and most interesting day when people run from shop to shop before Shabbat.

Artisanry

13) Nachalat Binyamin, the street of the "heirs of Theodor Herzl" (in Israel, Binyamin Herzl) is always good for a surprise. The audience is as diverse as the market itself: goldsmiths, potters, painters and other artists like street musicians, actors and fortune tellers exhibit their goods and services or simply themselves. There are plenty of opportunities to have a coffee and a snack in the neighboring cafés and bistros.
Tues.–Fri. 10.00–17.00 starting at Allenby St. /Nachalat Binyamin St.
http://www.nachalatbinyamin.com

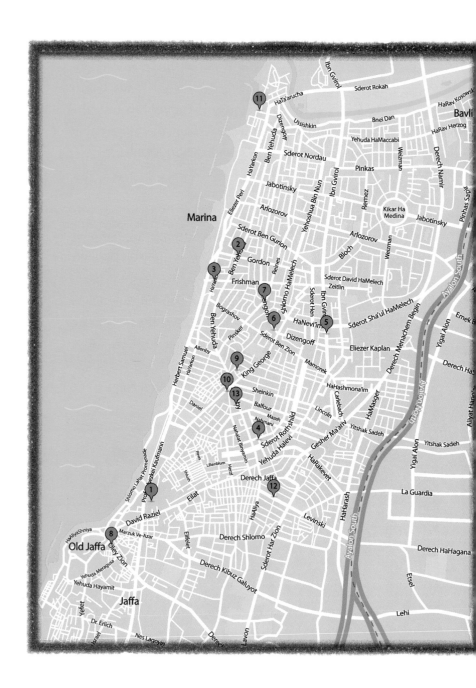

12

Accommodation

FINDING A GREAT HOTEL in Tel Aviv is not very difficult. The prices are in US-$ and any acceptable hotel starts at about $135 per night. Israel is a high-tech nation and an Internet connection is provided nearly everywhere you go. If you will require parking for your car, you should inquire about this with the hotel you are considering before you book. Parking space is very scarce in the city.

Consulting hotel websites is worth the while before booking even the flight. Many hotels offer discounts that are only good on certain days. Of course, you will also find major hotel chains like the Hilton or the Crowne Plaza.

Cancellation policies vary with each hotel and each season, especially during the Jewish holidays. Most tourists are not aware of this. Many hotels do not accept cancellations later than 48 hours before arrival. During the High Holidays, it is customary for many hotels that the whole stay has to be paid in advance and cancellations are not accepted later than 10 days before arrival.

The prices mentioned are the average price published by the hotels. Depending on the season, they might vary a lot.

12.1 Hotels

1) Sadot Hotel, Ben-Gurion Airport
http://www.atlas.co.il/sadot-hotel-tel-aviv
ca. $160–260/night
This airport hotel is not only a very comfortable solution when you have a night flight; this is the only Israeli hotel that has ever made it on the list of Expedia's best hotels of the world.

2) The Varsano Hotel
16 Hevrat Shas
http://thevarsano.com
ca. $350+/night
The Varsano offers exceptional suites in a historic area. Close to the old Jaffa train station (tachana), this hotel hides behind a little wooden door in the middle of the villagey Neve Tzedek while still being situated in the center of buzzing Tel Aviv. Cut off the outer world and have an unforgettable stay in the stylish and modern suites.

3) Brown TLV
25 Kalisher St.
http://www.browntlv.com
ca. $120–250/night
This hotel is still relatively new (opened end of 2010) but was soon renowned for its modern and elegant design together with nice features like iPod charging stations in the rooms. The in-house wellness offerings are far above average as is the charming roof terrace. A very good value for the money! The hotel is located in the very north of Neve Tzedek, a very lively part of Tel Aviv.

The Yemenite Quarter as well as the Rothschild Boulevard can be reached by foot.

4) Grand Beach Hotel

250 HaYarkon St.

http://www.grandhotels-israel.com

ca. $140–238/night

Like many other hotels in Tel Aviv, the Grand Beach Hotel also occupies a building from the 1960s. Behind the façade, you will discover a successfully refurbished nice place with a pool on the roof terrace. The Hilton Hotel is right next door as is the beach: 7 minutes from the room to the sand. The old port is only a stone's throw away.

5) The Diaghilev, LIVE ART Boutique Hotel

56 Mazeh St.

http://www.diaghilev.co.il

ca. $150–200/night

As the name suggests, this hotel is all about art. Every single one of the suites is a little art gallery of its own. The hotel is only one block away from famous Rothschild Boulevard and you can reach many sites by foot. This building in the International Style was built in 1934 by architects Josef & Ze'ev Berlin and served as the first headquarters of the newspaper Hearts that still exists today.

6) Center Chic Hotel

2 Zamenhoff St.

http://www.atlas.co.il/center-hotel-tel-aviv

ca. $160–250/night

It is hardly possible to be "more Tel Aviv" than this hotel. Breakfast is served in the Cinema Hotel on Dizengoff Square, a so-called

"Bauhaus building" that transports the guest to the bygone era of the 1930s, the time of the city's first architectural boom. With free bikes from the hotel, it is easy to explore the city. Later, you can come back for tea time on the roof terrace.

7) City Hotel
9 Mapu St.
http://www.atlas.co.il/city-hotel-tel-aviv
ca. $155–265/night
The City Hotel is a modern and nice place with a welcoming interior and comfort like all hotels of this chain. Located close to the beach above Dizengoff Square, from here you can discover the "White City" whose many representative buildings from the 1930s are also located in this area.

8) Cinema Hotel
1 Zamenhoff St.
http://www.atlas.co.il/cinema-hotel-tel-aviv
ca. $170–275/night
Like being in a movie! The Cinema Hotel is the "big brother" of the Center Chic Hotel and a must for cineastes. The architects Yehuda & Raphael built it in 1939 in the "International Style" of the 1930s. Before it became a hotel, it used to be home to the Esther Cinema which is the theme of the whole building: all decoration is movie-related.

9) Andromeda Hill
3 Louis Pasteur St. /38 Yefet St.
http://www.andromeda.co.il
ca. $180+/night
The Andromeda Hill is a truly upscale residence with a gym and

pool appealing to refined tastes; a world of its own, hidden from the very different Jaffa. Here, you have the opportunity to experience the Near East during your day outside and in the evening, you come back to the Occident.

10) Shalom Hotel & Relax Tel Aviv

216 HaYarkon St.

http://www.atlas.co.il/shalom-hotel-tel-aviv

ca. \$200–300/night

Shalom & Relax. Nomen est omen: Welcome to the start of your holiday! In the neighborhood of the marina as well as other upper-class hotels like Hilton, Crowne Plaza, etc., and the exclusive shops of the Northern Dizengoff. The roof top offers a wonderful view and a nice terrace.

11) Hotel Montefiore

36 Montefiore St.

http://www.hotelmontefiore.co.il

ca. $250+/night

This exclusive little boutique hotel hides in the heart of Tel Aviv. The building is from 1922 and shows the typical Eclectic Style from this period. This neighborhood was the first of the young Tel Aviv (Ahuzat Bayit). Strategically located between Rothschild Boulevard, Sheinkin Street and the Yemenite Quarter, you can walk anywhere from here. The style of the rooms is very welcoming in warm colors and decorated with works from young Israeli artists. Do not miss the cuisine of the hotel's restaurant!

12) Nina Suites Hotel

29 Shabazi St.

http://www.ninacafehotel.com

ca. $250+/night

Located in trendy Neve Tzedek, the hotel was founded by Eliza Zibi who is also the owner of the Nina Café on the other side of the street where breakfast is served. The suites are very cozy and at the same time, modern and elegant. The beach is a 10-minute walk away through this very picturesque neighborhood of Tel Aviv with low-rise buildings and red roofs.

13) Arbel Hotel Apartment

11 Hulda St.

http://www.israelapartment.com

ca. $100–180/night

Hulda Street is a quiet little street off Dizengoff, close to the exclusive hotel chains. The marina is only 10 minutes away and the old port with all its restaurants, bars and coffee shops is also close by. The apartments are of a practical interior and the guests want for nothing. All together good value for money.

12.2 Hostels

I F A HOTEL IS JUST not right for your budget or preference, you might want to consider a hostel where you can spend the night for about $25. Ear plugs should be part of your basic equipment. Most of the hostels offer a kitchen you can use and free Wi-Fi Internet. The breakfast is generally not worth mentioning (except for the Gordon Inn). They can all be booked via the established online portals.

14) Florentine Hostel
16 Elifelet St.
The Florentine is a typical backpacker place, age limit: 40. Located in the new-comer district of Florentin between Jaffa and Neve Tzedek in a rather industrial area where a lot of renovations are still going on. The hostel itself is a friendly, busy place where single travelers can also easily make new friends.

15) Old Jaffa Hostel
8 Oley Zion St., Jaffa
This hostel is legendary and the atmosphere is a very authentic reflection of life in Jaffa: busy and diverse. Close to the flea market, you will find this colorfully decorated house with a roof terrace where you can have your first coffee in the morning and sleep in a hammock at night (only during summer).

16) Gordon Inn
17 Gordon St.

The Gordon Inn is listed as a hostel as well as a hotel. As a hostel, it is fabulous. The big Israeli breakfast they serve every morning at 8.00 is included and that alone is worth the stay: hummus, trina, shakshuka and more. If you are Jewish and want matzot for Pessach, just ask (and you will be given). The building itself is from the 1960s, the furnishing functional and clean. The hostel is located between the beach and Dizengoff Street, above the Dizengoff Square. Also suitable for families!

17) Hayarkon 48
48 HaYarkon St.

The location is a killer: right behind the seafront, close to Allenby Street. It takes no longer than 4 minutes from the room to the beach. The hostel is quite big as is the kitchen, and you can do your laundry, use the TV room, the billiards or have a hot shower all day long. The breakfast consists of coffee, bread and jam. Around the corner, there are enough places to buy everything you need for a beautiful morning picnic at the sea.

18) Mugraby Hostel
19 Allenby St.

This hostel is very close to the beach and though it is very centrally located, it is possible to sleep at night. If you are not looking for a kitchen to use and still want a clean place for little money, the Mugraby is just fine.

19) Chef Hostel Montefiore
19 Montefiore St.

In all hostels you will easily find travelers like you, but the Chef

Hostel means "instant friendship." It is a bit more expensive than the average hostel but absolutely worth it. Many guests cook together in the open kitchen or have a beer in the charming back yard. Just off Allenby St., the Chef Hostel is run by a local family who will make you feel at home.

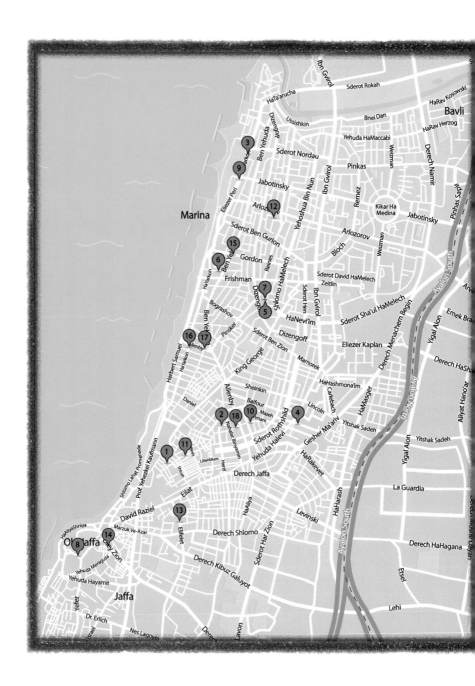